AN ANTHOLOGY
OF
MODERN VERSE

If thou indeed derive thy light from Heaven,
Then, to the measure of that heaven-born light,
Shine, Poet! in thy place, and be content:
The stars pre-eminent in magnitude,
And they that from the zenith dart their beams,
(Visible though they be to half the earth,
Though half a sphere be conscious of their bright-
    ness),
Are yet of no diviner origin,
No purer essence, than the one that burns,
Like an untended watch-fire on the ridge
Of some dark mountain ; or than those which seem
Humbly to hang, like twinkling winter lamps,
Among the branches of the leafless trees.

Wordsworth

AN ANTHOLOGY
OF
MODERN VERSE

Chosen *by* A. METHUEN

With an Introduction
by ROBERT LYND

"By nothing is England so glorious
as by her poetry"—MATTHEW ARNOLD

METHUEN & CO. LTD.
36 ESSEX STREET W.C.
LONDON

Twenty-eighth Edition

First Published, May 12th, 1921; Second and Third Editions, 1921; Fourth Edition (enlarged), 1921.
Fifth and Sixth (Thin Paper) Editions, 1921.
Seventh Edition, 1921; Eighth and Ninth Editions, 1922.
Tenth (Thin Paper) Edition, 1922.
Eleventh, Twelfth and Thirteenth Editions, 1923.
Fourteenth (Thin Paper) Edition, 1923.
Fifteenth and Sixteenth Editions, 1924.
Seventeenth (Thin Paper) Edition, 1924.
Eighteenth Edition, 1924.
Nineteenth (Thin Paper) Edition, 1925.
Twentieth Edition, 1925.
Twenty-first Edition, 1926.
Twenty-second Edition, 1927.
Twenty-third (Thin Paper) Edition, 1927.
Twenty-fourth Edition, 1929.
Twenty-fifth (Thin Paper) Edition, 1929.
Twenty-sixth Edition, 1930.
Twenty-seventh (Thin Paper) Edition, 1933.
Twenty-eighth Edition, 1934.

First School Edition, June 1921; Second and Third Editions, 1922; Fourth, Fifth and Sixth Editions, 1923; Seventh, Eighth and Ninth Editions, 1924; Tenth and Eleventh Editions, 1925; Twelfth and Thirteenth Editions, 1926; Fourteenth and Fifteenth Editions, 1927; Sixteenth and Seventeenth Editions, 1928; Eighteenth and Nineteenth Editions, 1929; Twentieth, Twenty-first and Twenty-second Editions, 1930; Twenty-third Edition, 1931; Twenty-fourth Edition, 1932; Twenty-fifth Edition, 1933.

TO
THOMAS HARDY, O.M.
GREATEST
OF THE MODERNS

CONTENTS

ON POETRY AND THE MODERN MAN

POETRY was born, like Beatrice, under a dancing star. There is in the nature of things a law of dancing which, at a crisis of great happiness or exaltation, sets the thoughts and the emotions leaping rhythmically to time. All men, even those who would be most surprised to be reckoned among the poets or the followers of the poets, are subject to this law. Every child is a poet from the age at which he learns to beat a silver spoon on the table in numbers. He likes to make not only a noise but a noise with something of the regularity of an echo. He coos with delight when he is taken on an elder's knee and is trotted up and down to the measure of " This is the way the ladies ride," with its steady advance of pace till the ultimate fury of the country clown's gallop. Later on, he himself trots gloriously in reins with bells that jingle in rhyme as he runs. His pleasure in swings, in sitting behind a horse, in travelling in a train, with its puff as regular as an uncle's watch and its wheels thudding out endless hexameters on the line, arise from the same delight in rhythm. We may even trace the origins of the poet in those first reduplications of sound that lead a child to call a train a puff-puff and its mother ma-ma. Cynics may pretend that it is nurses and foolish parents who invent the language of babyhood. It is the child, however, who feels that a sound does not mean enough till it has rhymed itself double, and who of its own accord will gravely murmur " cawr-cawr " to a scratching hen or " wow-wow " to a dog with expectant eyes and ears.

It is difficult to remember what was the first literature one enjoyed in childhood. But I feel reasonably certain that it was in rhyme. No child who ever lived in an old house, with a clock like a tall wooden tower beating the seconds at the turn of the stairs, but must have owed one of its first literary thrills to *Hickory-dickory-dock*. To know the rhyme was to live with a clock that might become a mouse's race-course. It made the stairs even more intensely exciting than they were before. It brought the patter of new hopes and fears into the house. The nursery-rhyme thrill, I think, precedes by a considerable time the prose thrill of *Jack the Giant-Killer*, and even in *Jack the Giant-Killer* it is when the Giant falls to rhyming with his—

> Fee-foh-fum,
> I smell the blood of an Englishman,

that the excitement catches fire. It is in verse that the imagination learns its first steps. The first sorrows with which we learn to sympathize in literature are the sorrows of Bo-peep. Our first sense of the comedy of disaster we owe to Jack and Jill. Into ethical comedy—the comedy brought to adult perfection by Molière—we were initiated at the hands of Little Jack Horner and Margery Daw. Reading and hearing the nursery-rhymes, indeed, we went round the entire clock-face of the emotions —at least of the emotions possible to a child. We were merry with Old King Cole, excited with Little Miss Muffet, distraught with the Old Woman who lived in a Shoe. We heard the bell toll for Cock Robin and stood by his grave. Crosspatch was as real to us as the face in the mirror. We opened the door into romance with a rhyme about a white horse and a woman who had rings on her fingers and bells on her toes. Critics of literature are fond of making a distinction between poetry and verse, and it is possible to make these distinctions in regard to nursery rhymes equally with every other kind of literature. If we must do so, I should say that, while *Little Miss Muffet* is indubitably verse and *Little Jack Horner* (though rich in character as in diet) almost indubitably so, *Ride a Cock-Horse* is poetry. Here we are in a fantastic world, a world beyond the prose of knowledge. *Polly, Put the Kettle On*, contains not a word or a rhyme that makes the world a new place for us. *Ride a Cock-Horse*, however, and *Mary, Mary, Quite Contrary*, carry us out of our walled lives like a dream. They liberate us into a fairyland of chiming music and flowers.

In poetry we are continually being re-born into new fairylands. The poet in the child is a traveller into fairyland, and if at a later stage he returns to reality, he must bring back with him fire from

that Heaven if he is to remain a poet. He cannot
be a poet of experience unless he has first been a
poet of innocence. Poetry begins as a random
voyage among the blue seas of fancy, though it
may end with the return of a laden treasure-ship
of the imagination into the harbours of home.
The poet of riper years cannot entirely dissociate
his imaginative life from his every-day experience.
He is always a commentator on life under whatever
disguises. The child, on the other hand, claims
complete liberty of the imagination, and can build
for itself at a moment's notice a world as perfect
and useless and beautiful as a soap-bubble—a
world in which defiance is bidden to all the zoologists
and geographers and gods of the things that are.
The child, it may be argued, is in this enjoying
the pleasure of inexperience rather than rebelling
against experience, and, perhaps, this gives us a clue
to one of the secrets of poetry. The poet must
always retain a mighty sense of inexperience—of
a world outside him of which he can know nothing
save by guesses and wonder. True poetry begins
with the delighted use of this sense. It creates
the mermaid, the unicorn and the fiery dragon. It
peoples the vague unknown with witches on broom-
sticks and fairies and beasts that are kings' sons in
disguise. Distance has no terrors for it, and we can
travel over impossible spaces either in seven-league
boots or by the light of a candle :

> " How many miles to Babylon ? "
> " Three score and ten."
> " Can I get there by candle-light ? "
> " Yes, and back again."

That is the poet's licence. Impossible trees bear

impossible fruits, and for their sake an impossible
princess comes over the sea :

> I had a little nut tree ;
>   Nothing would it bear,
> But a silver nutmeg
>   And a golden pear.
> The King of Spain's daughter
>   Came to visit me,
> And all because
>   Of my little nut tree.

You might easily construct a theory of poetry,
taking this most charming of nursery-songs as your
text.   Here, better than in many a more pompous
poem, you can see what it is that distinguishes
poetry from prose.   Here is the imagination escaping
from the four walls—laughing at the four walls—
and building its own house out of nothing but beauty
and rhymes.   Like all fine poetry, it is a thing of
pleasant sights and pleasant sounds—of images
and music.   Prose, too, can give us these delights.
But verse which gives them to us is what we speci-
fically call poetry.

For convenience' sake, however, most of us use
the word " poetry " with different meanings in
different contexts.   In one context we mean by it
verse that has taken the wings of inspiration, or
even prose that dares the same levels.   In another,
we mean simply literature in verse or in rhythms
akin to those of verse.   Whichever may be the
sense in which we use the word, there is a good
defence of poetry as, not the possession of a select
few, but a part of the general human inheritance.
Poetry is natural to man : it is not a mere cult of
abnormal or intellectual persons.   We see the beginnings of it, not only in the child's love of repetition

and rhythms and jingles, but in the scullery uses
to which verse is put by school-boys and grown men.
Boys and men take to verse for use as well as beauty.
We can remember the number of days in each month
better because of the rhyme that begins " Thirty
days hath September."

Milton, in his attack on rhyme, denounced the
" jingling sound of like endings," as though they
were but a child's toys that a mature world should
lay aside.   But the truth is that rhyme makes even
a fact doubly a fact because it makes it memorable.
Memorableness, after all, is one of the eminent
qualities in literature.   We judge the greatness of
an author largely by his genius for writing memorable
passages.   He must do more, but he must incident-
ally pass this test.   The appeal to the memory
seems to be part of the appeal to the imagination.
The memory desires patterns, whether of metre or
rhyme or alliteration, and the pattern in its turn
excites the imagination to make new and unexpected
uses of it.   Poetry has a double birth : it has a
utilitarian father and an æsthetic mother.   The man
who first said, " Birds of a feather flock together,"
was probably a teacher anxious to leave a lesson
that would repeat itself in the mind, but he also
seems to have been a little excited in his wisdom,
and so he gave us not only a pattern but an image.
We see the same use of the pattern as a net for the
image in the didactic poets.   Hesiod is a didactic
writer of verse, but, in the heat of his excitement,
he is exalted into an imaginative poet.   Lucretius
sought to make his philosophy memorable by putting
it into verse ; as he did so, his verse rose into poetry
that is more memorable than his philosophy.   I

do not wish to suggest that this literally was the way in which the masterpieces of Hesiod and Lucretius shaped themselves. I wish only to emphasize the fact that each of them wrote with the aid of two muses—a muse of utility and a muse of inspiration. Horace of the critical verse and Pope of the critical and moral verse also did so, though in different degrees. Wit and wisdom, no less than desire, seem to turn naturally to the poetic pattern. Pope has often been derided as a prosaic writer, but, if he had written in prose, he would not be one of the most frequently quoted of English authors. It was a muse, a muse, that sharpened his arrows. His epigrams may be as monotonous as soldiers in a battalion on the march, but like the soldiers, they have gained at least in neatness and deportment from the regimental discipline. The epigram in verse is not necessarily superior to the epigram in prose, but other things being equal, it seems to stamp itself deeper and more delightfully on the memory ; and lines such as

Willing to wound, and yet afraid to strike,

and

Mistress of herself, though China fall,

remain clear as gold pendants in the mind when the wittiest sayings of La Rochefoucauld and Dr. Johnson have become a little blurred. Even if we despised rhyme and metre as Tolstoy did, and held that nothing has been said in verse that could not be better said in prose, we should still have to admit that many things are said more permanently in verse. Great story-tellers, like great wits, have turned to verse, consciously or unconsciously, in

b

search of this permanence. In the result, Homer shows us the adventures of men from a higher tower than we are permitted to climb in even the most beautiful of prose tales such as those of the Irish heroes. Here the muse of utility and the muse of inspiration do not merely march side by side : they are no longer two but one.

So far the aim of my argument has been to suggest that in the past a taste for poetry has in some degree been natural to men in general ; first, because our emotions automatically seek to express themselves in patterns of rhythm and measure, and, secondly, because the memory finds such patterns useful as well as pleasant. On the score of memory, perhaps, the defence of poetry has weakened since the introduction of books and especially since the introduction of printing. Memory nowadays stores on the bookshelf many things that the memory of Homer's contemporaries had to store in the brain. Our memory is no longer our chief reference library. Hence the teacher of facts—agriculture, theology, or genealogies—has in recent centuries been ever less tempted to say what he has to say in verse. Verse that merely makes knowledge or opinion or anecdote tinkle no longer appeals to us, and to write a treatise on farming or botany in verse would in these days be to court ridicule. Wit can still triumph in verse in spite of a lack of the poetic fire ; but, on the whole, it is true of the modern man who reads verse that he is descended not from the jingler of facts and wise saws, but from the enraptured child beating the spoon on the table.

At every great hour of his life—hours of passionate

happiness or passionate sorrow—if he can speak at all, he is aware of the futility of common speech. His deepest personal emotions find no echo in the prose of a leading article or in the intonations of the commercial traveller discussing the short-comings of provincial hotels. He feels as inarticulate as though he had never learned to speak. He may be a fluent conversationalist, but in presence of love and death he is dumb. He is not contentedly dumb, however. His dumbness is but a prelude to a longing for utterance. He realizes that while speech has given him words that make him master of the common objects in his house, it has as yet given him no words to express what he has begun to perceive or half-perceive in this vast house of the universe in which he finds himself a visitor. He is like a man invited to the king's table who knows only the language of the shop and the servants' hall. To experience any of the deeper emotions of life—whether in love, religion, patriotism, or the desire for a more perfect world—is to be a guest of the king, and the language of the king is, in the finer sense of the word, poetry. We realize that the room in which we have so far been content to live is mean and narrow, and even though we return to it, it can no longer confine us like a prison, but is rich with memories that enable us to escape at will into the sense of that unforgettable experience. We do this either by becoming poets ourselves or by becoming poets by proxy. Poetry is that which reminds us of reality, and that we live in a world, not merely of twenty-four-hour days, but of great occasions.

The function of poetry is to make the life of

Mare's phrase—is the beginning of poetry, whether
in the nursery or the grown man. It may be the
longing of love or the longing for God or the longing
merely for some permanence somewhere in a world
of things that pass like the wind and disappear into
the earth like snow. Whitman relates in *Out of the
Cradle Endlessly Rocking* how his whole life was
changed by hearing, as a boy, the song of a bird
breaking its heart in longing for its lost mate.
" Now I know what I am for," he cries :

Nevermore shall I escape, nevermore the reverberations,
Nevermore the cries of unsatisfied love be absent from me.
Never again leave me to be the peaceful child I was before
    what, there, in the night
By the sea, under the yellow and sagging moon,
The messenger there aroused—the fire, the sweet hell
    within,
The unknown want, the destiny of me.

Without that " unknown want " there would be
no poetry.

Sir Henry Newbolt in an admirable essay treats
poetry as a transfiguration of life heightened by the
home-sickness of the spirit for a perfect world ; and
it would be difficult to find a more suggestive theory
in contemporary criticism. The home-sickness of
the poet may be home-sickness for beauty, or for
permanence, or even for the past. The home-sickness of Mr. Hardy differs from the home-sickness
of Mr. Yeats, and the home-sickness of Mr. Davies
from the home-sickness of Mr. de la Mare. But there
is this element in each of them, making them all
equally, if not equal, poets. In the absence of it,
man is but a prodigal, glad to be allowed to live
on the husks, without memory of his father's house.
At the same time, " home-sickness " is not altogether

the best word to express this longing of the spirit. It has a connotation of plaintiveness that does not seem to accord with the hunger for reality of a Browning or the hunger for God of an A. E. A. E., it is true, called his first book of verse *Homeward : Songs by the Way* ; but they are songs of a spirit, not sick, but eager for home. On the other hand, all those sad poets who chiefly mourn over the transience of things may justly be defined as homesick, though some of them are home-sick for a home that they believe does not exist.

Of all contemporary poets, there is none who is so obviously the poet of home-sickness as Mr. de la Mare. He is the poet of " love shackled with vain-longing "—vain-longing for lovely things that pass, for love that passes. He draws consolation, however, from the fact that, though things pass, they pass in a perpetuity of beauty. The stream remains though it does not stand still—the stream of lovely things that change, watched by loving eyes that change. Hence he bids us :

> Look thy last on all things lovely
> Every hour. Let no night
> Seal thy sense in deathly slumber
> Till to delight
> Thou have paid thy utmost blessing ;
> Since that all things thou would'st praise
> Beauty took from those who loved them
> In other days.

Every poet continually returns to the stream of lovely things—the stream that flows and yet remains. This is for him the river of life—the brook that flows " fast by the oracle of God." His attitude to it may vary from the delight of the soul in the Creator of these deep and incessant waters to the delight of the eye in the play of wind or the skimming of a blue-backed swallow over its surface. But, whatever his attitude to it, he knows that without it the world would be an Egypt without a Nile. He may not be conscious of the reason why he is homesick for its banks. A Browning and a Swinburne, a Hardy and a Yeats, haunt its shores for reasons that seem defiantly contradictory of each other. But all of them alike know that but for its waters we should be inhabitants of a barren plain—that here is what gives life riches and significance. That is why men must always return to poetry. Civilized human beings cannot be content to live like desert tribesmen, ignorant of what it is that makes life significant and rich. They live under a constant pressure of mechanical needs, like animals and savages. But even the fullest satisfaction of these needs leaves them only animals and savages. They must have something else—the something else that makes man a master, that satisfies his hunger for reality. The poets, like the religious teachers, the historians, and the astronomers, help to satisfy this hunger. We may live opposite to an advertisement hoarding and be overwhelmed by a sense of the visible commonness of things; but Mr. Davies will transform the world back into the likeness of reality with an image of a waterfall. He will do more for us than this. Even when we live, not among advertisement hoardings, but among green and singing things, we are creatures of indolent and occasional sight and hearing. To read him is to see with new eyes, to hear with new

ears. He invites us to a more intense experience
of eye and ear than we have before known. Like
Mr. de la Mare, he bids us look on all things lovely
as longingly as though it were for the last time.

> A rainbow and a cuckoo's song
> May never come together again.

Perhaps, however, one could define the different
qualities of Mr. de la Mare's and Mr. Davies's poetry
better by saying that, while Mr. de la Mare has the
genius for making us look on lovely things as though
for the last time, Mr. Davies has a gift for making
us look at them as if for the first time. When we
read his poem on the robin:

> That little hunchback in the snow,

we feel as if we had never perfectly seen a robin
before.

The variety of the poems in the present anthology
—an anthology that gives a better idea of the diffuse
and ubiquitous riches of recent poetry than any
that has yet appeared—should help to remind any
thoughtful reader that we must always look for
personal differences of this sort as among the essen-
tial things in poetry. Every poet extends the boun-
daries of reality for us; but he is not the master
of all reality; he makes but a partial and personal
conquest. He is not a teacher, telling us the significance of all significant things. He can reveal only
those things that were significant to himself. To
Mr. Hardy the ship of which we read in *A Passer-By*
would not have been superlatively significant as
it was to Mr. Bridges. To Mr. Bridges the forlorn
figures in *Beyond the Last Lamp* would not have

been superlatively significant as they were to Mr.
Hardy. Mr. Squire is as incapable of the original
imaginative experience recorded in Mr. Yeats's
The Song of Wandering Aengus as Mr. Yeats is of
the original imaginative experience recorded in Mr.
Squire's *Winter Nightfall*. Every poet has his own
net and his own draught of fishes. Even when
we have invented a formula that seems to explain
those things the poets have in common, we shall
find that each of them escapes out of the formula
and has to be re-formulated—or, as I should prefer
to say, portrayed—in terms of his own personality.
Each of them has even a personal music, and the
musical characteristics of the poets are as clearly
distinguishable as are those of Mozart and Bach
and Chopin. This does not necessarily imply
the invention of new forms. Mr. Yeats can take
the rhymed couplet, as in *The Folly of Being Comforted*, and he can make of it something new—a
measure unknown alike to Pope and to Keats.
Not that Mr. Yeats has been slow to invent new
forms, as in several of the poems in *The Wind
Among the Reeds*. But many of these are merely
variations of well-known forms, as when he trans-
forms the quatrain of four beats to magic uses
in *Had I the Heaven's Embroidered Cloths*. Mr.
Bridges, like Mr. Yeats, has made music hitherto
unknown in both old and new measures. *A
Passer-By* is written in a form as original as
those poems in which he is merely experiment-
ing in metre. In it he has intermixed the
beat of dactyl and spondee in a music that
lesser poets have imitated but greater poets had
not anticipated. Mr. Hardy has not influenced

the rhythm of recent verse as Mr. Bridges and
Mr. Yeats have, but he, too, loves to experiment
with new forms. At the same time, some of his
most unforgettable poems, such as *The Oxen* and
In Time of " The Breaking of Nations," are poems
in which he makes use of old and simple metres.
Among the younger poets of distinction, none has
shown himself more impatient of the settled forms
than Mr. Squire. He has taken over the cultivated
dactyl of Mr. Bridges, as in *August Moon* and *A
Far Place,* but he has used it in rhythms that have
a new flow. His long practice as one of the wittiest
parodists of his time compelled him, I suspect, to
turn away from forms in which he had learned too
thoroughly the habit of imitation. As a result,
though a mocker of " free verse," he has claimed
some of the liberties of " free verse," as in that
beautiful poem *The Stronghold.*

On the whole, however, as any reader of the
present anthology can see, though there has been
a continuous invention of new forms on the part
of living and recent writers, the good poets of the
twentieth century have not been nearly so revolu-
tionary either in form or in formlessness as is sometimes imagined. The notion of what is correct in
rhyme has changed, largely owing to the influence
of Mr. de la Mare, whose occasional half-rhymes
are a part of the charm of his music. We find the
later Mr. Yeats deliberately rhyming " did " and
" head." But there are precedents for these faint
rhymes even in the most consciously musical of
the Elizabethans, Campion. Wilfred Owen made
a further innovation with his consonantal rhymes
and wrote a whole poem in which the lines ended

irony is a protest that seeks us out and punishes us. The truth is, there has never been a greater variety of moods among poets than during the past two generations. The poets of war may be regarded as a group by themselves; but even among them what has Mr. Sassoon, or even Mr. Nichols, in common with Grenfell and the Rupert Brooke who wrote:

Now, God be thanked Who has matched us with His
   hour;

and:

   If I should die, think only this of me:
      That there's some corner of a foreign field
   That is for ever England.

The Georgian group of poets are frequently regarded as a single school. They have been censured in the mass as " the week-end school of poetry," as though they were writers on themes rather than poets under compulsion. One may disagree with this criticism, but one can see the point of it. More poetry is written to-day in a rapture of self-consciousness than in the selfless rapture of a Shelley. Poetry of the sensibilities is commoner than poetry of the passions. The passion of love sets as few of the younger poets on fire as the passion of politics. The only great book of love poetry written in English by a living man is Mr. Yeats' *Wind Among the Reeds*. There are great individual lyrics of love, such as Mr. Bridges' *Awake, my Heart, to be Loved*; but nothing so matchless has been written in this mood by any of the younger men. You have only to compare the present anthology with any good collection of Elizabethan verse in order to see how love has dwindled as a theme for poetry. The absence of political passion from modern verse is more easily understood. Politics as a rule make bad poetry, but I am not sure that they are not a part of the make-up of great poets. Wordsworth and Byron and Shelley were all ardent politicians, and that generous ardour, I am convinced, enriched their imaginative lives. Mr. Squire, it is true, has written a witty book of political passion, *The Survival of the Fittest*. But, for the most part, the poets have been not only dumb but indifferent in a world in which there is an unprecedented need for the creative imagination in politics. Whether the deepening social consciousness that has come into the world in the last century and a half will ever become the common stuff of poetry is, I admit, doubtful. Great poetry is not the expression of collective feeling. It is the speech of soul to soul. On the other hand, as Whitman showed in *To a Foil'd European Revolutionaire*, there is room for the expression of personal passion in politics as in religion. No one is eager to see the poets turning aside from the Muse to tell us that " a man's a man for a' that." But it is reasonable to believe that Burns's genial realization that " a man's a man for a' that " was of service to him as a poet in that it made him a richer-natured human being. Modern poetry has its own genius, however,* and we need

* Those who are inclined to condemn modern poetry because it does not square with some pre-established code, would do well to remember what Wordsworth said in regard to the appreciation of poetry of a new kind in his introduction to *Lyrical Ballads*. " Readers accustomed to the gaudiness and inane phraseology of many modern writers," wrote Wordsworth, " if they persist in reading this book to its conclusion, will perhaps frequently have to struggle with feelings of strangeness and awkwardness ; they will look round for poetry, and will be induced to enquire by what species of courtesy these attempts

not weigh it against that of another age as we delight
in its sensibility, its wealth of observation, its conquest of new themes, its perpetual rediscovery of
simple things and of their effect on the consciousness.

We may see in it, as in the poetry of the Lake
school, a revolt against convention in favour of
reality.   As in the verse of the Lake school, the
thing seen has become more important than the
thing said.   The twentieth century is recovering
from too much Tennyson as the nineteenth century
had to recover from too much Pope.   Tennyson,
no doubt, has often been praised for his minute
observation of nature, but it is not as a familiar
of nature that he survives as a poet.   He was a
lord of the literary manner and the æstheticism
of the nineties came as logically after him as after
Rossetti and Swinburne.   The Georgian poets, like
the Lake poets, are re-establishing the claim of
familiar experiences to poetical treatment in familiar
language.   They love birds like naturalists rather
than æsthetes.

> To him this must have been a familiar sight,

is the epitaph Mr. Hardy foresees for himself, as he
watches the hawk alighting on the " wind-warped

---

can be permitted to assume that title. It is desirable that
such readers, for their own sakes, should not suffer the solitary
word Poetry, a word of very disputed meaning, to stand in
the way of their gratification ; but that, while they are perusing
this book, they should ask themselves if it contains a natural
delineation of human passions, human characters, and human
incidents ; and if the answer be favourable to the author's
wishes, that they should consent to be pleased in spite of that
most dreadful enemy to our pleasures, our own pre-established
codes of decision."

upland thorn " at the close of evening.   There is almost more of the spirit of John Clare than of Wordsworth in the modern eagerness to set down exactly some small individual experience as a thing of value in itself.   Mr. de la Mare, it is true, is no naturalist ; he even goes so far over the borders of romance as to give the blackbird " golden shoon." Mr. Davies is more representative of one of the tendencies of modern poetry when he exclaims :

> I could sit down here alone
> And count the oak-trees one by one.

We find this surrender to the immediate joy of the eye, not only in Mr. Hardy and Mr. Bridges, but in most of the younger poets, down even to such meditative writers as Mr. Freeman and Mr. Brett Young.   It is as though poetry were now going through the same phase of evolution that painting went through in the days of Impressionism. The same passion for the actual, for the record of the minutiæ of personal experience, accounts perhaps for the frequency of place-names in contemporary poetry.   Gloucestershire means something to Mr. Drinkwater, Sussex to Mr. Belloc, that was never expressed in Elizabethan or eighteenth-century poetry.

Poetry, if not politics, has succeeded in taking us back to the land, and the exiles in the towns return home.   We are aware of this even in the work of so romantic a poet as Mr. Turner : he returns in his imagination to a more giant world under lonelier stars, as Dora Sigerson and Moira O'Neill return to the soft rains of Ireland.

c

And side by side with this return to the roads of home there are evidences that something like a return to religion is in progress. We see signs of this, not only in such Catholic poets as Mr. Chesterton and Mrs. Meynell, but in the work of Mr. Gould, Mr. Graves and Mrs. Shove. Painting to-day has gone to the café, but poetry lingers at the door of the church. In this, I think, poetry is more faithful to the tradition of the arts. For what is art but a consolation of exiles by the waters of Babylon? As I have said, however, it is in vain that we make categories for the poets, if we expect them to be mechanically perfect and beyond contradiction. We can point to a few tendencies, like currents in the sea, but winds blow across from the east and the west, and the tide makes for a thousand shores. The moon and her rule are still the same. What is most important in modern poetry is not that which distinguishes it from the poetry of yesterday, but that which makes it in its degree one with the poetry of Homer and Sappho, of Shakespeare and Shelley.

Critical opinion is still conflicting as to the place to which the various poets represented in this anthology will ultimately be entitled in the hierarchy of authors. Mr. Bridges and Mr. Hardy, Mr. Yeats and Mr. Davies have all been the subjects of widely different estimates. There are critics—and able critics—who would like to arrange the poets in order (first, second, third, etc.), like horses at the end of a race. This, I think, is only a minor function of criticism. We must, indeed, have a standard by which we know, without even the trouble of thinking, that Flecker is a lesser poet than Milton.

But our pleasure in reading Wordsworth does not consist in knowing that he is a greater poet than Keats, or our pleasure in Keats in knowing that he is greater than Wordsworth, either of these judgments being reasonably tenable by a good critic. The good critic is he who can define a poet's genius in terms of quality rather than in terms of quantity. The astronomer must know the greater and lesser magnitudes of the stars ; but the stars have more exciting interests than these. When Wordsworth wrote :

> If thou indeed derive thy light from Heaven . . .
>   Shine, Poet, in thy place and be content,

he was bequeathing a lesson not only to poets but to critics. Mr. Hardy and Mr. Bridges, Mr. Yeats and Mr. Davies may well be content to know that they are luminaries for all time ; and even many of the smaller poets in this collection may be well enough pleased to be peeps of light in a not inglorious constellation. That there is no Shakespeare writing in our midst is a fact in support of which it is unnecessary to argue. But our generation has not failed to add new and lovely lights to the firmament. The poets of to-day are not a remnant but a nation. That is the justification—if justification were needed —of this fine and catholic collection of modern verse. In an age poor in poets a miscellany of such varied excellences would be impossible.

ROBERT LYND

COMPILER'S NOTE

THE compiler renders his sincere thanks to those authors and publishers whose names are mentioned in the index of authors and whose kindness has made this selection possible. Considerations of copyright have prevented the inclusion of poems by one or two eminent writers.

There is an obvious difficulty in deciding where modern verse begins, but, roughly, the pieces chosen for this book are either the work of living poets or, with rare exceptions, of poets who have died within the last fifteen years. It is hoped in any case that the spirit of the new poetry inspires this little book.

January, 1921

Eighteen new pieces, each marked ⁴ in the Index of Authors, have been added to the Fourth Edition.

August, 1921

PUBLISHERS' NOTE
TO TWENTY-SEVENTH EDITION

OWING to the revisions which living poets are tempted from time to time to introduce into their work, the text of the poems in any modern anthology is likely to differ from other texts in the reader's possession. In this edition of *An Anthology of Modern Verse*, the poems have all been collated with versions published under the authors' names, and therefore present a text which has at some time been approved by them or their literary executors.

January, 1933

AN INDEX OF AUTHORS

[The numeral on the left denotes the Edition in which a new piece appeared.]

AN ANTHOLOGY

OF

MODERN VERSE

FROLIC

THE children were shouting together
  And racing along the sands,
A glimmer of dancing shadows,
  A dovelike flutter of hands.

The stars were shouting in heaven,
  The sun was chasing the moon :
The game was the same as the children's,
  They danced to the self-same tune.

The whole of the world was merry,
  One joy from the vale to the height,
Where the blue woods of twilight encircled
  The lovely lawns of the light.

A. E.

BABYLON

THE blue dusk ran between the streets : my love
  was winged within my mind,
It left to-day and yesterday and thrice a thousand
  years behind.

To-day was past and dead for me, for from to-day
    my feet had run
Through thrice a thousand years to walk the ways of
    ancient Babylon.
On temple top and palace roof the burnished gold
    flung back the rays
Of a red sunset that was dead and lost beyond a
    million days.
The tower of heaven turns darker blue, a starry
    sparkle now begins ;
The mystery and magnificence, the myriad beauty
    and the sins
Come back to me. I walk beneath the shadowy
    multitude of towers ;
Within the gloom the fountain jets its pallid mist in
    lily flowers.
The waters lull me and the scent of many gardens,
    and I hear
Familiar voices, and the voice I love is whispering
    in my ear.
Oh real as in dream all this ; and then a hand on
    mine is laid :
The wave of phantom time withdraws ; and that
    young Babylonian maid,
One drop of beauty left behind from all the flowing
    of that tide,
Is looking with the self-same eyes, and here in
    Ireland by my side.
Oh light our life in Babylon, but Babylon has taken
    wings,
While we are in the calm and proud procession of
    eternal things.

A. E.

HYMN TO LOVE

WE are thine, O Love, being in thee and made of
 thee,
 As thou, Love, were the deep thought
And we the speech of the thought; yea, spoken
 are we,
 Thy fires of thought out-spoken:

But burn'd not through us thy imagining
 Like fierce mood in a song caught,
We were as clamour'd words a fool may fling,
 Loose words, of meaning broken.

For what more like the brainless speech of a fool,—
 The lives travelling dark fears,
And as a boy throws pebbles in a pool
 Thrown down abysmal places?

Hazardous are the stars, yet is our birth
 And our journeying time theirs;
As words of air, life makes of starry earth
 Sweet soul-delighted faces;

As voices are we in the worldly wind;
 The great wind of the world's fate
Is turned, as air to a shapen sound, to mind
 And marvellous desires.

But not in the world as voices storm-shatter'd,
 Not borne down by the wind's weight;
The rushing time rings with our splendid word
 Like darkness fill'd with fires.

For Love doth use us for a sound of song,
  And Love's meaning our life wields,
Making our souls like syllables to throng
    His tunes of exultation.

Down the blind speed of a fatal world we fly,
  As rain blown along earth's fields;
Yet are we god-desiring liturgy,
    Sung joys of adoration;

Yea, made of chance and all a labouring strife,
  We go charged with a strong flame;
For as a language Love hath seized on life
    His burning heart to story.

Yea, Love, we are thine, the liturgy of thee,
  Thy thought's golden and glad name,
The mortal conscience of immortal glee,
    Love's zeal in Love's own glory.

Lascelles Abercrombie

PRAYERS

God who created me
  Nimble and light of limb,
In three elements free,
  To run, to ride, to swim:
Not when the sense is dim,
  But now from the heart of joy,
I would remember Him:
  Take the thanks of a boy.

Jesu, King and Lord,
  Whose are my foes to fight,

Gird me with Thy sword,
  Swift and sharp and bright.
Thee would I serve if I might,
  And conquer if I can ;
From day-dawn till night,
  Take the strength of a man.

Spirit of Love and Truth,
  Breathing in grosser clay,
The light and flame of youth,
  Delight of men in the fray,
Wisdom in strength's decay ;
  From pain, strife, wrong to be free,
This best gift I pray,
  Take my spirit to Thee.

Henry Charles Beeching

THE SOUTH COUNTRY

WHEN I am living in the Midlands
  That are sodden and unkind,
I light my lamp in the evening :
  My work is left behind ;
And the great hills of the South Country
  Come back into my mind.

The great hills of the South Country
  They stand along the sea ;
And it's there walking in the high woods
  That I could wish to be,
And the men that were boys when I was a boy
  Walking along with me.

The men that live in North England
   I saw them for a day;
Their hearts are set upon the waste fells,
   Their skies are fast and grey;
From their castle-walls a man may see
   The mountains far away.

The men that live in West England
   They see the Severn strong,
A-rolling on rough water brown
   Light aspen leaves along.
They have the secret of the Rocks
   And the oldest kind of song.

But the men that live in the South Country
   Are the kindest and most wise,
They get their laughter from the loud surf,
   And the faith in their happy eyes
Comes surely from our Sister the Spring
   When over the sea she flies;
The violets suddenly bloom at her feet,
   She blesses us with surprise.

I never get between the pines
   But I smell the Sussex air;
Nor I never come on a belt of sand
   But my home is there.
And along the sky the line of the Downs
   So noble and so bare.

A lost thing could I never find,
   Nor a broken thing mend:
And I fear I shall be all alone
   When I get towards the end.
Who will there be to comfort me
   Or who will be my friend?

I will gather and carefully make my friends
  Of the men of the Sussex Weald;
They watch the stars from silent folds,
  They stiffly plough the field.
By them and the God of the South Country
  My poor soul shall be healed.

If I ever become a rich man,
  Or if ever I grow to be old,
I will build a house with deep thatch
  To shelter me from the cold,
And there shall the Sussex songs be sung
  And the story of Sussex told.

I will hold my house in the high wood
  Within a walk of the sea,
And the men that were boys when I was a boy
  Shall sit and drink with me.

               Hilaire Belloc

DUNCTON HILL

He does not die that can bequeath
Some influence to the land he knows,
Or dares, persistent, interwreath
Love permanent with the wild hedgerows;
  He does not die, but still remains
  Substantiate with his darling plains.

The spring's superb adventure calls
His dust athwart the woods to flame;
His boundary river's secret falls
Perpetuate and repeat his name.
  He rides his loud October sky:
  He does not die. He does not die.

The beeches know the accustomed head
Which loved them, and a peopled air
Beneath their benediction spread
Comforts the silence everywhere;
    For native ghosts return and these
    Perfect the mystery in the trees.

So, therefore, though myself be crosst
The shuddering of that dreadful day
When friend and fire and home are lost
And even children drawn away—
    The passer-by shall hear me still,
    A boy that sings on Duncton Hill.

Hilaire Belloc

THE BIRDS

WHEN Jesus Christ was four years old,
The angels brought Him toys of gold,
Which no man ever had bought or sold.

And yet with these He would not play.
He made Him small fowl out of clay,
And blessed them till they flew away:
    Tu creasti, Domine.

Jesus Christ, Thou child so wise,
Bless mine hands and fill mine eyes,
And bring my soul to Paradise.

Hilaire Belloc

FOR THE FALLEN

WITH proud thanksgiving, a mother for her children,
  England mourns for her dead across the sea.
Flesh of her flesh they were, spirit of her spirit,
  Fallen in the cause of the free.

Solemn the drums thrill : Death august and royal
  Sings sorrow up into immortal spheres.
There is music in the midst of desolation
  And a glory that shines upon our tears.

They went with songs to the battle, they were young,
  Straight of limb, true of eye, steady and aglow.
They were staunch to the end against odds un-
    counted,
  They fell with their faces to the foe.

They shall grow not old, as we that are left grow old :
  Age shall not weary them, nor the years condemn.
At the going down of the sun and in the morning
  We will remember them.

They mingle not with their laughing comrades again ;
  They sit no more at familiar tables of home ;
They have no lot in our labour of the day-time ;
  They sleep beyond England's foam.

But where our desires are and our hopes profound,
  Felt as a well-spring that is hidden from sight,
To the innermost heart of their own land they are
    known
  As the stars are known to the Night ;

As the stars that shall be bright when we are dust,
  Moving in marches upon the heavenly plain,
As the stars that are starry in the time of our
    darkness,
    To the end, to the end, they remain.

Laurence Binyon

O WORLD, BE NOBLER

O World, be nobler, for her sake !
  If she but knew thee, what thou art,
What wrongs are borne, what deeds are done
In thee, beneath thy daily sun,
  Know'st thou not that her tender heart
For pain and very shame would break ?
O World, be nobler, for her sake !

Laurence Binyon

ALMSWOMEN

At Quincey's moat the squandering village ends,
And there in the almshouse dwell the dearest friends
Of all the village, two old dames that cling
As close as any trueloves in the spring.
Long, long ago they passed threescore-and-ten,
And in this doll's house lived together then ;
All things they have in common, being so poor,
And their one fear, Death's shadow at the door.
Each sundown makes them mournful, each sunrise
Brings back the brightness in their failing eyes.

How happy go the rich fair-weather days
When on the roadside folk stare in amaze
At such a honeycomb of fruit and flowers
As mellows round their threshold ; what long hours
They gloat upon their steepling hollyhocks,
Bee's balsams, feathery southernwood, and stocks,
Fiery dragon's-mouths, great mallow leaves
For salves, and lemon-plants in bushy sheaves,
Shagged Esau's-hands with five green finger-tips.
Such old sweet names are ever on their lips.
As pleased as little children where these grow
In cobbled pattens and worn gowns they go,
Proud of their wisdom when on gooseberry shoots
They stuck eggshells to fright from coming fruits
The brisk-billed rascals ; pausing still to see
Their neighbour owls saunter from tree to tree,
Or in the hushing half-light mouse the lane
Long-winged and lordly.
                          But when these hours wane,
Indoors they ponder, scared by the harsh storm
Whose pelting saracens on the window swarm,
And listen for the mail to clatter past
And church clock's deep bay withering on the blast ;
They feed the fire that flings a freakish light
On pictured kings and queens grotesquely bright,
Platters and pitchers, faded calendars
And graceful hour-glass trim with lavenders.

Many a time they kiss and cry, and pray
That both be summoned in the selfsame day,
And wiseman linnet tinkling in his cage
End too with them the friendship of old age,
And all together leave their treasured room
Some bell-like evening when the may's in bloom.
                                    Edmund Blunden

THE BARN

RAIN-SUNKEN roof, grown green and thin
For sparrows' nests and starlings' nests;
Dishevelled eaves; unwieldly doors,
Cracked rusty pump, and oaken floors,
And idly-pencilled names and jests
     Upon the posts within.

The light pales at the spider's lust,
The wind tangs through the shattered pane:
An empty hop-poke spreads across
The gaping frame to mend the loss
And keeps out sun as well as rain,
     Mildewed with clammy dust.

The smell of apples stored in hay
And homely cattle-cake is there.
Use and disuse have come to terms,
The walls are hollowed out by worms,
But men's feet keep the mid-floor bare
     And free from worse decay.

All merry noise of hens astir
Or sparrows squabbling on the roof
Comes to the barn's broad open door;
You hear upon the stable floor
Old hungry Dapple strike his hoof,
     And the blue fan-tail's whir.

The barn is old, and very old,
But not a place of spectral fear.
Cobwebs and dust and speckling sun
Come to old buildings every one.
Long since they made their dwelling here,
     And here you may behold

Nothing but simple wane and change;
Your tread will wake no ghost, your voice
Will fall on silence undeterred.
No phantom wailing will be heard,
Only the farm's blithe cheerful noise;
    The barn is old, not strange.

Edmund Blunden

THE OLD SQUIRE

I LIKE the hunting of the hare
    Better than that of the fox;
I like the joyous morning air,
    And the crowing of the cocks.

I like the calm of the early fields,
    The ducks asleep by the lake,
The quiet hour which Nature yields,
    Before mankind is awake.

I like the pheasants and feeding things
    Of the unsuspicious morn;
I like the flap of the wood-pigeon's wings
    As she rises from the corn.

I like the blackbird's shriek, and his rush
    From the turnips as I pass by,
And the partridge hiding her head in a bush,
    For her young ones cannot fly.

I like these things, and I like to ride,
    When all the world is in bed,
To the top of the hill where the sky grows wide,
    And where the sun grows red.

A great storm from the ocean goes shouting o'er
the hill,
  And there is glory in it and terror on the wind,
But the haunted air of twilight is very strange
and still,
  And the little winds of twilight are dearer to my
mind.

The great waves of the Atlantic sweep storming on
their way,
  Shining green and silver with the hidden herring
shoal,
But the Little Waves of Breffny have drenched
my heart in spray,
  And the Little Waves of Breffny go stumbling
through my soul.

Eva Gore Booth

NEW YEAR'S EVE, 1913

O, CARTMEL bells ring soft to-night,
  And Cartmel bells ring clear,
But I lie far away to-night,
  Listening with my dear;

Listening in a frosty land
  Where all the bells are still
And the small-windowed bell-towers stand
  Dark under heath and hill.

I thought that, with each dying year,
  As long as life should last
The bells of Cartmel I should hear
  Ring out an aged past:

The plunging, mingling sounds increase
  Darkness's depth and height,
The hollow valley gains more peace
  And ancientness to-night :

The loveliness, the fruitfulness,
  The power of life lived there
Return, revive, more closely press
  Upon that midnight air.

But many deaths have place in men
  Before they come to die ;
Joys must be used and spent, and then
  Abandoned and passed by.

Earth is not ours ; no cherished space
  Can hold us from life's flow,
That bears us thither and thence by ways
  We knew not we should go.

O, Cartmel bells ring loud, ring clear,
  Through midnight deep and hoar,
A year new-born, and I shall hear
  The Cartmel bells no more.

                     Gordon Bottomley

TO IRON-FOUNDERS AND OTHERS

WHEN you destroy a blade of grass
  You poison England at her roots :
Remember no man's foot can pass
  Where evermore no green life shoots.

You force the birds to wing too high
  Where your unnatural vapours creep :
Surely the living rocks shall die
  When birds no rightful distance keep.

  2

You have brought down the firmament,
  And yet no heaven is more near;
You shape huge deeds without event,
  And half made men believe and fear.

Your worship is your furnaces,
  Which, like old idols, lost obscenes,
Have molten bowels; your vision is
  Machines for making more machines.

O, you are busied in the night,
  Preparing destinies of rust;
Iron misused must turn to blight
  And dwindle to a tettered crust.

The grass, forerunner of life, has gone:
  But plants that spring in ruins and shards
Attend until your dream is done:
  I have seen hemlock in your yards.

The generations of the worm
  Know not your loads piled on their soil;
Their knotted ganglions shall wax firm
  Till your strong flagstones heave and toil.

When the old hollowed earth is cracked,
  And when, to grasp more power and feasts,
Its ores are emptied, wasted, lacked,
  The middens of your burning beasts

Shall be raked over till they yield
  Last priceless slags for fashionings high,
Ploughs to wake grass in every field,
  Chisels men's hands to magnify.

Gordon Bottomley

LIGHT

THE night has a thousand eyes,
    And the day but one;
Yet the light of the bright world dies
    With the dying sun.

The mind has a thousand eyes,
    And the heart but one;
Yet the light of a whole life dies
    When love is done.

F. W. Bourdillon

SO SWEET LOVE SEEMED

So sweet love seemed that April morn,
When first we kissed beside the thorn,
So strangely sweet, it was not strange
We thought that love could never change.

But I can tell—let truth be told—
That love will change in growing old;
Though day by day is naught to see,
So delicate his motions be.

And in the end 'twill come to pass
Quite to forget what once he was,
Nor even in fancy to recall
The pleasure that was all in all.

His little spring, that sweet we found,
So deep in summer floods is drowned,
I wonder, bathed in joy complete,
How love so young could be so sweet.

Robert Bridges

AWAKE, MY HEART, TO BE LOVED

AWAKE, my heart, to be loved, awake, awake !
The darkness silvers away, the morn doth break,
It leaps in the sky : unrisen lustres slake
The o'ertaken moon. Awake, O heart, awake !

She too that loveth awaketh and hopes for thee ;
Her eyes already have sped the shades that flee,
Already they watch the path thy feet shall take :
Awake, O heart, to be loved, awake, awake !

And if thou tarry from her,—if this could be,—
She cometh herself, O heart, to be loved, to thee ;
For thee would unashamèd herself forsake :
Awake to be loved, my heart, awake, awake !

Awake ! the land is scattered with light, and see,
Uncanopied sleep is flying from field and tree :
And blossoming boughs of April in laughter shake ;
Awake, O heart, to be loved, awake, awake !

Lo all things wake and tarry and look for thee :
She looketh and saith, " O sun, now bring him to me.
Come more adored, O adored, for his coming's sake,
And awake my heart to be loved : awake, awake ! "

Robert Bridges

I WILL NOT LET THEE GO

I WILL not let thee go.
Ends all our month-long love in this ?
    Can it be summed up so,
    Quit in a single kiss ?
I will not let thee go.

I will not let thee go.
If thy words' breath could scare thy deeds,
As the soft south can blow
And toss the feathered seeds,
Then might I let thee go.

I will not let thee go.
Had not the great sun seen, I might;
Or were he reckoned slow
To bring the false to light,
Then might I let thee go.

I will not let thee go.
The stars that crowd the summer skies
Have watched us so below
With all their million eyes,
I dare not let thee go.

I will not let thee go.
Have we not chid the changeful moon,
Now rising late, and now
Because she set too soon,
And shall I let thee go?

I will not let thee go.
Have not the young flowers been content,
Plucked ere their buds could blow,
To seal our sacrament?
I cannot let thee go.

I will not let thee go.
I hold thee by too many bands:
Thou sayest farewell, and lo!
I have thee by the hands,
And will not let thee go.

Robert Bridges

A PASSER-BY

Whither, O splendid ship, thy white sails crowding,
  Leaning across the bosom of the urgent West,
That fearest nor sea rising, nor sky clouding,
  Whither away, fair rover, and what thy quest?
  Ah! soon, when Winter has all our vales opprest,
When skies are cold and misty, and hail is hurling,
  Wilt thou glide on the blue Pacific, or rest
In a summer haven asleep, thy white sails furling?

I there before thee, in the country that well thou
      knowest,
  Already arrived am inhaling the odorous air:
I watch thee enter unerringly where thou goest,
  And anchor queen of the strange shipping there,
  Thy sails for awnings spread, thy masts bare;
Nor is aught from the foaming reef to the snow-
      capp'd, grandest
  Peak, that is over the feathery palms more fair
Than thou, so upright, so stately, and still thou
      standest.

And yet, O splendid ship, unhailed and nameless,
  I know not if, aiming a fancy, I rightly divine
That thou hast a purpose joyful, a courage blame-
      less,
  Thy port assured in a happier land than mine.
  But for all I have given thee, beauty enough is
      thine,
As thou, aslant with trim tackle and shrouding,
  From the proud nostril curve of a prow's line
In the offing scatterest foam, thy white sails crowd-
      ing.

                                        Robert Bridges

THE LINNET

I HEARD a linnet courting
 His lady in the spring :
His mates were idly sporting,
 Nor stayed to hear him sing
  His song of love—
I fear my speech distorting
  His tender love.

One phrase was all his pleading,
 He spoke of love and home :
To her who gave him heeding
 He sang his question, " Come."—
  His gay sweet notes,
So sadly marred in the reading !
  His tender notes !

And when he ceased, the hearer
 Re-echoed the refrain,
And swiftly perching nearer,
 " Come, come," she sang again,—
  Ah for their loves !
Would that my verse spake clearer,
  Their tender loves !

Blest union of twin creatures
 Unmarred by sense of doubt :
All summer's dry misfeatures
 Such springtide trust bars out ;
  But of their loves
Fall short our wiser natures :
  Their tender loves !

       Robert Bridges

THE SOLDIER

IF I should die, think only this of me :
   That there's some corner of a foreign field
That is for ever England.   There shall be
   In that rich earth a richer dust concealed ;
A dust whom England bore, shaped, made aware,
   Gave, once, her flowers to love, her ways to roam,
A body of England's, breathing English air,
   Washed by the rivers, blest by suns of home.

And think, this heart, all evil shed away,
   A pulse in the eternal mind, no less
      Gives somewhere back the thoughts by Eng-
         land given ;
Her sights and sounds ; dreams happy as her day ;
   And laughter, learnt of friends ; and gentleness,
      In hearts at peace, under an English heaven.
                                        Rupert Brooke

THE DEAD

THESE hearts were woven of human joys and cares,
   Washed marvellously with sorrow, swift to mirth.
The years had given them kindness.   Dawn was
      theirs,
   And sunset, and the colours of the earth.
These had seen movement, and heard music ; known
   Slumber and waking ; loved ; gone proudly
      friended ;
Felt the quick stir of wonder ; sat alone ;
   Touched flowers and furs and cheeks.   All this
      is ended.

There are waters blown by changing winds to
    laughter
And lit by the rich skies, all day. And after,
   Frost, with a gesture, stays the waves that dance
And wandering loveliness. He leaves a white
   Unbroken glory, a gathered radiance,
A width, a shining peace, under the night.

                            Rupert Brooke

THE OLD VICARAGE, GRANTCHESTER

         Café des Westens, Berlin, May 1912
JUST now the lilac is in bloom,
All before my little room;
And in my flower-beds, I think,
Smile the carnation and the pink;
And down the borders, well I know,
The poppy and the pansy blow . . .
Oh! there the chestnuts, summer through,
Beside the river make for you
A tunnel of green gloom, and sleep
Deeply above; and green and deep
The stream mysterious glides beneath,
Green as a dream and deep as death.—
Oh, damn! I know it! and I know
How the May fields all golden show,
And when the day is young and sweet,
Gild gloriously the bare feet
That run to bathe . . .
              Du lieber Gott!

Here am I, sweating, sick, and hot,
And there the shadowed waters fresh
Lean up to embrace the naked flesh.

Temperamentvoll German Jews
Drink beer around ; and *there* the dews
Are soft beneath a morn of gold.
Here tulips bloom as they are told ;
Unkempt about those hedges blows
An English unofficial rose ;
And there the unregulated sun
Slopes down to rest when day is done,
And wakes a vague unpunctual star,
A slippered Hesper ; and there are
Meads towards Haslingfield and Coton
Where *das Betreten's* not *verboten* . . .
εἴθε γενοίμην . . . would I were
In Grantchester, in Grantchester !—
Some, it may be, can get in touch
With Nature there, or Earth, or such.
And clever modern men have seen
A Faun a-peeping through the green,
And felt the Classics were not dead,
To glimpse a Naiad's reedy head,
Or hear the Goat-foot piping low . . .
But these are things I do not know.
I only know that you may lie
Day long and watch the Cambridge sky,
And, flower-lulled in sleepy grass,
Hear the cool lapse of hours pass,
Until the centuries blend and blur
In Grantchester, in Grantchester . . .
Still in the dawnlit waters cool
His ghostly Lordship swims his pool,
And tries the strokes, essays the tricks,
Long learnt on Hellespont, or Styx.
Dan Chaucer hears his river still
Chatter beneath a phantom mill.

Tennyson notes, with studious eye,
How Cambridge waters hurry by . . .
And in that garden, black and white,
Creep whispers through the grass all night;
And spectral dance, before the dawn,
A hundred Vicars down the lawn;
Curates, long dust, will come and go
On lissom, clerical, printless toe;
And oft between the boughs is seen
The sly shade of a Rural Dean . . .
Till, at a shiver in the skies,
Vanishing with Satanic cries,
The prim ecclesiastic rout
Leaves but a startled sleeper-out,
Grey heavens, the first bird's drowsy calls,
The falling house that never falls.

God! I will pack, and take a train,
And get me to England once again!
For England's the one land, I know,
Where men with Splendid Hearts may go;
And Cambridgeshire, of all England,
The shire for Men who Understand;
And of *that* district I prefer
The lovely hamlet Grantchester.
For Cambridge people rarely smile,
Being urban, squat, and packed with guile;
And Royston men in the far South
Are black and fierce and strange of mouth;
At Over they fling oaths at one,
And worse than oaths at Trumpington,
And Ditton girls are mean and dirty,
And there's none in Harston under thirty,
And folks in Shelford and those parts,
Have twisted lips and twisted hearts,

And Barton men make cockney rhymes,
And Coton's full of nameless crimes,
And things are done you'd not believe
At Madingley, on Christmas Eve.
Strong men have run for miles and miles
When one from Cherry Hinton smiles;
Strong men have blanched and shot their wives
Rather than send them to St. Ives;
Strong men have cried like babes, bydam,
To hear what happened at Babraham.
But Grantchester! ah, Grantchester!
There's peace and holy quiet there,
Great clouds along pacific skies,
And men and women with straight eyes,
Lithe children lovelier than a dream,
A bosky wood, a slumbrous stream,
And little kindly winds that creep
Round twilight corners, half asleep.
In Grantchester their skins are white,
They bathe by day, they bathe by night;
The women there do all they ought;
The men observe the Rules of Thought.
They love the Good; they worship Truth;
They laugh uproariously in youth;
(And when they get to feeling old,
They up and shoot themselves, I'm told). . . .

Ah God! to see the branches stir
Across the moon at Grantchester!
To smell the thrilling-sweet and rotten,
Unforgettable, unforgotten
River-smell, and hear the breeze
Sobbing in the little trees.
Say, do the elm-clumps greatly stand,
Still guardians of that holy land?

The chestnuts shade, in reverend dream,
The yet unacademic stream ?
Is dawn a secret shy and cold
Anadyomene, silver-gold ?
And sunset still a golden sea
From Haslingfield to Madingley ?
And after, ere the night is born,
Do hares come out about the corn ?
Oh, is the water sweet and cool,
Gentle and brown, above the pool ?
And laughs the immortal river still
Under the mill, under the mill ?
Say, is there Beauty yet to find ?
And Certainty ? and Quiet kind ?
Deep meadows yet, for to forget
The lies, and truths, and pain ? . . . oh ! yet
Stands the Church clock at ten to three ?
And is there honey still for tea ?

Rupert Brooke

THE GREAT LOVER

I HAVE been so great a lover : filled my days
So proudly with the splendour of Love's praise,
The pain, the calm, and the astonishment,
Desire illimitable, and still content,
And all dear names men use, to cheat despair,
For the perplexed and viewless streams that bear
Our hearts at random down the dark of life.
Now, ere the unthinking silence on that strife
Steals down, I would cheat drowsy Death so far,
My night shall be remembered for a star
That outshone all the suns of all men's days.
Shall I not crown them with immortal praise

Whom I have loved, who have given me, dared with
    me
High secrets, and in darkness knelt to see
The inenarrable godhead of delight ?
Love is a flame ;—we have beaconed the world's
    night.
A city :—and we have built it, these and I.
An emperor :—we have taught the world to die.
So, for their sakes I loved, ere I go hence,
And the high cause of Love's magnificence,
And to keep loyalties young, I'll write those names
Golden for ever, eagles, crying flames,
And set them as a banner, that man may know,
To dare the generations, burn, and blow
Out on the winds of Time, shining and streaming. . . .

These I have loved :

        White plates and cups, clean-gleaming,
Ringed with blue lines ; and feathery, faery dust ;
Wet roofs, beneath the lamp-light; the strong crust
Of friendly bread ; and many-tasting food ;
Rainbows ; and the blue bitter smoke of wood ;
And radiant raindrops couching in cool flowers ;
And flowers themselves, that sway through sunny
    hours,
Dreaming of moths that drink them under the moon ;
Then, the cool kindliness of sheets, that soon
Smooth away trouble ; and the rough male kiss
Of blankets ; grainy wood ; live hair that is
Shining and free ; blue-massing clouds ; the keen
Unpassioned beauty of a great machine ;
The benison of hot water ; furs to touch ;
The good smell of old clothes ; and other such—
The comfortable smell of friendly fingers,
Hair's fragrance, and the musty reek that lingers
About dead leaves and last year's ferns. . . .

Dear names,
And thousand other throng to me ! Royal flames ;
Sweet water's dimpling laugh from tap or spring ;
Holes in the ground ; and voices that do sing ;
Voices in laughter, too ; and body's pain,
Soon turned to peace ; and the deep-panting train ;
Firm sands ; the little dulling edge of foam
That browns and dwindles as the wave goes home ;
And washen stones, gay for an hour ; the cold
Graveness of iron ; moist black earthen mould ;
Sleep ; and high places ; footprints in the dew ;
And oaks ; and brown horse-chestnuts, glossy-new ;
And new-peeled sticks ; and shining pools on
        grass ;—
All these have been my loves. And these shall pass,
Whatever passes not, in the great hour,
Nor all my passion, all my prayers, have power
To hold them with me through the gate of Death.
They'll play deserter, turn with the traitor breath,
Break the high bond we made, and sell Love's trust
And sacramented covenant to the dust.
—Oh, never a doubt but, somewhere, I shall wake,
And give what's left of love again, and make
New friends, now strangers. . . .
                        But the best I've known,
Stays here, and changes, breaks, grows old, is blown
About the winds of the world, and fades from brains
Of living men, and dies.
                        Nothing remains.

O dear my loves, O faithless, once again
This one last gift I give : that after men
Shall know, and later, lovers, far-removed,
Praise you, " All these were lovely " ; say, " He
        loved."
                                Rupert Brooke

OPIFEX

As I was carving images from clouds,
   And tinting them with soft ethereal dyes
   Pressed from the pulp of dreams, one comes, and
      cries :—
" Forbear ! " and all my heaven with gloom en-
      shrouds.

" Forbear !   Thou hast no tools wherewith to essay
   The delicate waves of that elusive grain :
   Wouldst have due recompense of vulgar pain ?
The potter's wheel for thee, and some coarse clay !

" So work, if work thou must, O humbly skilled !
   Thou hast not known the Master ; in thy soul
   His spirit moves not with a sweet control ;
Thou art outside, and art not of the guild."

Thereat I rose, and from his presence passed,
   But, going, murmured :—" To the God above,
   Who holds my heart, and knows its store of love
I turn from thee, thou proud iconoclast."

Then on the shore God stooped to me, and said :—
   " He spake the truth : even so the springs are set
   That move thy life, nor will they suffer let,
Nor change their scope ; else, living, thou wert
      dead.

" This is thy life : indulge its natural flow,
   And carve these forms. They yet may find a
      place
   On shelves for them reserved.   In any case,
I bid thee carve them, knowing what I know."

T. E. Brown

SWEET BREEZE

SWEET breeze that sett'st the summer buds a-sway-
    ing,
Dear lambs amid the primrose meadows playing,
Let me not think!
O floods, upon whose brink
The merry birds are maying,
Dream, softly dream! O blessed mother, lead me
Unsevered from thy girdle—lead me! feed me!
I have no will but thine;
I need not but the juice
Of elemental wine—
Perish remoter use
Of strength reserved for conflict yet to come!
Let me be dumb,
As long as 1 may feel thy hand—
This, this is all—do ye not understand
How the great Mother mixes all our bloods?
O breeze! O swaying buds!
O lambs, O primroses, O floods!

T. E. Brown

MY GARDEN

A GARDEN is a lovesome thing, God wot!
Rose plot,
Fringed pool,
Ferned grot—
The veriest school
Of peace; and yet the fool
Contends that God is not—
Not God! in gardens! when the eve is cool?
Nay, but I have a sign;
'Tis very sure God walks in mine.

T. E. Brown

3

DORA

SHE knelt upon her brother's grave,
   My little girl of six years old—
He used to be so good and brave,
   The sweetest lamb of all our fold;
He used to shout, he used to sing,
Of all our tribe the little king—
And so unto the turf her ear she laid,
To hark if still in that dark place he played.
No sound! no sound!
Death's silence was profound;
And horror crept
Into her aching heart, and Dora wept.
If this is as it ought to be,
My God, I leave it unto Thee.

T. E. Brown

I AM THE GILLY OF CHRIST

I AM the gilly of Christ,
   The mate of Mary's Son;
I run the roads at seeding time,
   And when the harvest's done.

I sleep among the hills,
   The heather is my bed;
I dip the termon-well for drink,
   And pull the sloe for bread.

No eye has ever seen me,
   But shepherds hear me pass,
Singing at fall of even
   Along the shadowed grass.

The beetle is my bellman,
   The meadow-fire my guide,
The bee and bat my ambling nags
   When I have need to ride.

All know me only the Stranger,
  Who sits on the Saxon's height ;
He burned the bacach's little house
  On last Saint Brigid's Night.

He sups off silver dishes,
  And drinks in a golden horn,
But he will wake a wiser man
  Upon the Judgment Morn !

I am the gilly of Christ,
  The mate of Mary's Son ;
I run the roads at seeding time,
  And when the harvest's done.

The seed I sow is lucky,
  The corn I reap is red,
And whoso sings the " Gilly's Rann "
  Will never cry for bread.

Joseph Campbell

THE DONKEY

WHEN fishes flew and forests walked
  And figs grew upon thorn,
Some moment when the moon was blood
  Then surely I was born ;

With monstrous head and sickening cry
  And ears like errant wings,
The devil's walking parody
  On all four-footed things.

The tattered outlaw of the earth,
  Of ancient crooked will ;
Starve, scourge, deride me : I am dumb,
  I keep my secret still.

Fools! For I also had my hour;
  One far fierce hour and sweet:
There was a shout about my ears,
  And palms before my feet.

G. K. Chesterton

THE HOUSE OF CHRISTMAS

THERE fared a mother driven forth
  Out of an inn to roam;
In the place where she was homeless
  All men are at home.
The crazy stable close at hand,
With shaking timber and shifting sand,
Grew a stronger thing to abide and stand
  Than the square stones of Rome.

For men are homesick in their homes,
  And strangers under the sun,
And they lay their heads in a foreign land
  Whenever the day is done.
Here we have battle and blazing eyes,
And chance and honour and high surprise,
But our homes are under miraculous skies
  Where the yule tale was begun.

A child in a foul stable,
  Where the beasts feed and foam;
Only where He was homeless
  Are you and I at home;
We have hands that fashion and heads that know,
But our hearts we lost—how long ago!—
In a place no chart nor ship can show
  Under the sky's dome.

This world is wild as an old wives' tale,
  And strange the plain things are,
The earth is enough and the air is enough
  For our wonder and our war ;
But our rest is as far as the fire-drake swings,
And our peace is put in impossible things
Where clashed and thundered unthinkable wings
  Round an incredible star.

To an open house in the evening
  Home shall men come,
To an older place than Eden
  And a taller town than Rome ;
To the end of the way of the wandering star,
To the things that cannot be and that are,
To the place where GOD was homeless
  And all men are at home.

               G. K. Chesterton

LEPANTO

WHITE founts falling in the Courts of the sun,
And the Soldan of Byzantium is smiling as they run ;
There is laughter like the fountains in that face of
    all men feared,
It stirs the forest darkness, the darkness of his
    beard,
It curls the blood-red crescent, the crescent of his
    lips,
For the inmost sea of all the earth is shaken with
    his ships.
They have dared the white republics up the capes
    of Italy,
They have dashed the Adriatic round the Lion of
    the Sea,

And the Pope has cast his arms abroad for agony
    and loss,
And called the kings of Christendom for swords
    about the Cross.
The cold queen of England is looking in the glass;
The shadow of the Valois is yawning at the Mass;
From evening isles fantastical rings faint the Spanish
    gun,
And the Lord upon the Golden Horn is laughing
    in the sun.

Dim drums throbbing, in the hills half heard,
Where only on a nameless throne a crownless prince
    has stirred,
Where, risen from a doubtful seat and half at-
    tainted stall,
The last knight of Europe takes weapons from the
    wall,
The last and lingering troubadour to whom the
    bird has sung,
That once went singing southward when all the
    world was young.
In that enormous silence, tiny and unafraid,
Comes up along a winding road the noise of the
    Crusade,
Strong gongs groaning as the guns boom far,
Don John of Austria is going to the war,
Stiff flags straining in the night-blasts cold
In the gloom black-purple, in the glint old-gold,
Torchlight crimson on the copper kettle-drums,
Then the tuckets, then the trumpets, then the can-
    non, and he comes.
Don John laughing in the brave beard curled,
Spurning of his stirrups like the thrones of all the
    world,

Holding his head up for a flag of all the free,
Love-light of Spain—hurrah!
Death-light of Africa!
Don John of Austria
Is riding to the sea.

Mahound is in his paradise above the evening star,
(*Don John of Austria is going to the war.*)
He moves a mighty turban on the timeless houri's
  knees,
His turban that is woven of the sunsets and the seas.
He shakes the peacock gardens as he rises from
  his ease,
And he strides among the tree-tops and is taller
  than the trees,
And his voice through all the garden is a thunder
  sent to bring
Black Azrael and Ariel and Ammon on the wing.
Giants and the Genii,
Multiplex of wing and eye,
Whose strong obedience broke the sky
When Solomon was king.

They rush in red and purple from the red clouds
  of the morn,
From temples where the yellow gods shut up their
  eyes in scorn;
They rise in green robes roaring from the green
  hells of the sea
Where fallen skies and evil hues and eyeless creatures be;
On them the sea-valves cluster and the grey sea-
  forests curl,
Splashed with a splendid sickness, the sickness of
  the pearl;

They swell in sapphire smoke out of the blue
    cracks of the ground,—
They gather and they wonder and give worship to
    Mahound.
And he saith, "Break up the mountains where
    the hermit-folk can hide,
And sift the red and silver sands lest bone of saint
    abide,
And chase the Giaours flying night and day, not
    giving rest,
For that which was our trouble comes again out
    of the west.
We have set the seal of Solomon on all things under
    sun,
Of knowledge and of sorrow and endurance of
    things done ;
But a noise is in the mountains, in the mountains,
    and I know
The voice that shook our palaces—four hundred
    years ago :
It is he that saith not 'Kismet'; it is he that
    knows not Fate ;
It is Richard, it is Raymond, it is Godfrey in the
    gate !
It is he whose loss is laughter when he counts the
    wager worth :
Put down your feet upon him, that our peace be
    on the earth."
For he heard drums groaning and he heard guns jar,
(*Don John of Austria is going to the war.*)
Sudden and still—hurrah !
Bolt from Iberia !
Don John of Austria
Is gone by Alcalar.

St. Michael's on his Mountain in the sea-roads of
 the north,
(*Don John of Austria is girt and going forth.*)
Where the grey seas glitter and the sharp tides shift
And the sea-folk labour and the red sails lift.
He shakes his lance of iron and he claps his wings
 of stone ;
The noise is gone through Normandy ; the noise
 is gone alone ;
The North is full of tangled things and texts and
 aching eyes,
And dead is all the innocence of anger and surprise,
And Christian killeth Christian in a narrow dusty
 room,
And Christian dreadeth Christ that hath a newer
 face of doom,
And Christian hateth Mary that God kissed in Galilee,
But Don John of Austria is riding to the sea.
Don John calling through the blast and the eclipse,
Crying with the trumpet, with the trumpet of his lips,
Trumpet that sayeth ha !
 Domino gloria !
Don John of Austria
Is shouting to the ships.

King Philip's in his closet with the Fleece about
 his neck,
(*Don John of Austria is armed upon the deck.*)
The walls are hung with velvet that is black and
 soft as sin,
And little dwarfs creep out of it and little dwarfs
 creep in.
He holds a crystal phial that has colours like the
 moon,
He touches, and it tingles, and he trembles very soon,

OUR LADY

MOTHER of God ! no lady thou :
   Common woman of common earth !
Our Lady ladies call thee now,
   But Christ was never of gentle birth ;
   A common man of the common earth.

For God's ways are not as our ways.
   The noblest lady in the land
Would have given up half her days,
   Would have cut off her right hand,
   To bear the child that was God of the land.

Never a lady did He choose,
   Only a maid of low degree,
So humble she might not refuse
   The carpenter of Galilee.
   A daughter of the people, she.

Out she sang the song of her heart.
   Never a lady so had sung.
She knew no letters, had no art ;
   To all mankind, in woman's tongue,
   Hath Israelitish Mary sung.

And still for men to come she sings,
   Nor shall her singing pass away.
" *He hath filled the hungry with good things* "—
   Oh, listen, lords and ladies gay !—
   " *And the rich He hath sent empty away.*"

Mary E. Coleridge

AN OLD WOMAN OF THE ROADS

Oh, to have a little house!
  To own the hearth and stool and all!
The heaped-up sods upon the fire,
  The pile of turf against the wall!

To have a clock with weights and chains
  And pendulum swinging up and down,
A dresser filled with shining delph,
  Speckled and white and blue and brown!

I could be busy all the day
  Clearing and sweeping hearth and floor,
And fixing on their shelf again
  My white and blue and speckled store!

I could be quiet there at night
  Beside the fire and by myself,
Sure of a bed, and loth to leave
  The ticking clock and the shining delph!

Och! but I'm weary of mist and dark,
  And roads where there's never a house or bush,
And tired I am of bog and road
  And the crying wind and the lonesome hush!

And I am praying to God on high,
  And I am praying Him night and day,
For a little house, a house of my own—
  Out of the wind's and the rain's way.

                              Padraic Colum

NON NOBIS, DOMINE

Not unto us, O Lord,
Not unto us the rapture of the day,
The peace of night, or love's divine surprise,
High heart, high speech, high deeds 'mid honouring
    eyes ;
For at Thy word
All these are taken away.

Not unto us, O Lord :
To us Thou givest the scorn, the scourge, the scar,
The ache of life, the loneliness of death,
The insufferable sufficiency of breath.
And with Thy sword
Thou piercest very far.

Not unto us, O Lord ;
Nay, Lord, but unto her be all things given.
May light and life and earth and sky be blasted,
But let not all that wealth of loss be wasted ;
Let Hell afford
The pavement of her Heaven !

Henry Cust

IN ROMNEY MARSH

As I went down to Dymchurch Wall,
    I heard the South sing o'er the land :
I saw the yellow sunlight fall
    On knolls where Norman churches stand.

And ringing shrilly, taut and lithe,
    Within the wind a core of sound,
The wire from Romney town to Hythe
    Alone its airy journey wound.

A veil of purple vapour flowed
   And trailed its fringe along the Straits;
The upper air like sapphire glowed;
   And roses filled Heaven's central gates.

Masts in the offing wagged their tops;
   The swinging waves pealed on the shore;
The saffron beach, all diamond drops
   And beads of surge, prolonged the roar.

As I came up from Dymchurch Wall,
   I saw above the Downs' low crest
The crimson brands of sunset fall,
   Flicker and fade from out the west.

Night sank: like flakes of silver fire
   The stars in one great shower came down;
Shrill blew the wind; and shrill the wire
   Rang out from Hythe to Romney town.

The darkly shining salt sea drops
   Streamed as the waves clashed on the shore;
The beach, with all its organ stops.
   Pealing again, prolonged the roar.
                John Davidson

A CINQUE PORT

BELOW the down the stranded town
   What may betide forlornly waits,
With memories of smoky skies,
   When Gallic navies crossed the straits;
When waves with fire and blood grew bright,
And cannon thundered through the night.

4

With swinging stride the rhythmic tide
 Bore to the harbour barque and sloop ;
Across the bar the ship of war,
 In castled stern and lanterned poop,
Came up with conquests on her lee,
The stately mistress of the sea.

Where argosies have wooed the breeze,
 The simple sheep are feeding now ;
And near and far across the bar
 The ploughman whistles at the plough ;
Where once the long waves washed the shore,
Larks from their lowly lodgings soar.

Below the down the stranded town
 Hears far away the rollers beat ;
About the wall the seabirds call ;
 The salt wind murmurs through the street ;
Forlorn the sea's forsaken bride
Awaits the end that shall betide.

       John Davidson

PIPER, PLAY !

Now the furnaces are out,
 And the aching anvils sleep ;
Down the road the grimy rout
 Tramples homeward, twenty deep.
  Piper, play ! Piper, play !
   Though we be o'erlaboured men,
  Ripe for rest, pipe your best !
   Let us foot it once again !

Bridled looms delay their din ;
  All the humming wheels are spent ;
Busy spindles cease to spin ;
  Warp and woof must rest content.
    Piper, play ! Piper, play !
      For a little we are free !
      Foot it, girls, and shake your curls,
        Haggard creatures though we be !

Racked and soiled the faded air
  Freshens in our holiday ;
Clouds and tides our respite share ;
  Breezes linger by the way.
    Piper, rest ! Piper, rest !
      Now, a carol of the moon !
      Piper, piper, play your best !
        Melt the sun into your tune!

We are of the humblest grade ;
  Yet we dare to dance our fill :
Male and female were we made—
  Fathers, mothers, lovers still !
    Piper—softly ; soft and low ;
      Pipe of love in mellow notes,
      Till the tears begin to flow
        And our hearts are in our throats.

Nameless as the stars of night
  Far in galaxies unfurled,
Yet we wield unrivalled might,
  Joints and hinges of the world !
    Night and day ! night and day !
      Sound the song the hours rehearse !
    Work and play ! work and play !
      The order of the universe !

Now the furnaces are out,
  And the aching anvils sleep;
Down the road a merry rout
  Dances homeward, twenty deep.
    Piper, play! Piper, play!
      Wearied people though we be,
    Ripe for rest, pipe your best!
      For a little we are free!

John Davidson

WHERE SHE IS NOW

WHERE she is now, I cannot say—
  The world has many a place of light;
Perhaps the sun's eyelashes dance
  On hers, to give them both delight.

Or does she sit in some green shade,
  And then the air that lies above
Can with a hundred pale blue eyes
  Look through the leaves and find my love.

Perhaps she dreams of life with me,
  Her cheek upon her finger-tips;
O that I could leap forward now,
  Behind her back, and, with my lips,

Break through those curls above her nape,
  That hover close and lightly there;
To prove if they are substance, or
  But shadows of her lovely hair.

W. H. Davies

LEISURE

WHAT is this life if, full of care,
We have no time to stand and stare.

No time to stand beneath the boughs
And stare as long as sheep and cows.

No time to see, when woods we pass,
Where squirrels hide their nuts in grass.

No time to see, in broad daylight,
Streams full of stars, like skies at night.

No time to turn at Beauty's glance,
And watch her feet, how they can dance.

No time to wait till her mouth can
Enrich that smile her eyes began.

A poor life this if, full of care,
We have no time to stand and stare.

W. H. Davies

THE KINGFISHER

IT was the Rainbow gave thee birth,
  And left thee all her lovely hues;
And, as her mother's name was Tears,
  So runs it in thy blood to choose
For haunts the lonely pools, and keep
In company with trees that weep.

Go you and, with such glorious hues,
　　Live with proud Peacocks in green parks;
On lawns as smooth as shining glass,
　　Let every feather show its mark;
Get thee on boughs and clap thy wings
Before the windows of proud kings.

Nay, lovely Bird, thou art not vain;
　　Thou hast no proud ambitious mind;
I also love a quiet place
　　That's green, away from all mankind;
A lonely pool, and let a tree
Sigh with her bosom over me.

W. H. Davies

RICH DAYS

WELCOME to you rich Autumn days,
　　Ere comes the cold, leaf-picking wind;
When golden stooks are seen in fields,
　　All standing arm-in-arm entwined;
And gallons of sweet cider seen
On trees in apples red and green.

With mellow pears that cheat our teeth,
　　Which melt that tongues may suck them in;
With cherries red, and blue-black plums,
　　Now sweet and soft from stone to skin;
And woodnuts rich, to make us go
Into the loneliest lanes we know.

W. H. Davies

A GREAT TIME

Sweet Chance, that led my steps abroad,
  Beyond the town, where wild flowers grow—
A rainbow and a cuckoo, Lord,
  How rich and great the times are now!
      Know, all ye sheep
      And cows, that keep
On staring that I stand so long
  In grass that's wet from heavy rain—
A rainbow and a cuckoo's song
  May never come together again;
      May never come
      This side the tomb.

                              W. H. Davies

EARLY SPRING

How sweet this morning air in spring,
  When tender is the grass, and wet!
I see some little leaves have not
  Outgrown their curly childhood yet;
And cows no longer hurry home,
However sweet a voice cries " Come."

Here, with green Nature all around,
  While that fine bird the skylark sings;
Who now in such a passion is,
  He flies by it, and not his wings;
And many a blackbird, thrush and sparrow
Sing sweeter songs that I may borrow.

These watery swamps and thickets wild—
    Called Nature's slums—to me are more
Than any courts where fountains play,
    And men-at-arms guard every door;
For I could sit down here alone,
And count the oak-trees one by one.

                                    W. H. Davies

THE MOON

THY beauty haunts me heart and soul,
    Oh thou fair Moon, so close and bright;
Thy beauty makes me like the child,
    That cries aloud to own thy light:
The little child that lifts each arm
To press thee to her bosom warm.

Though there are birds that sing this night
    With thy white beams across their throats,
Let my deep silence speak for me
    More than for them their sweetest notes:
Who worships thee till music fails,
Is greater than thy nightingales.

                                    W. H. Davies

SILVER

SLOWLY, silently, now the moon
Walks the night in her silver shoon;
This way, and that, she peers, and sees
Silver fruit upon silver trees;
One by one the casements catch
Her beams beneath the silvery thatch;

Couched in his kennel, like a log,
With paws of silver sleeps the dog;
From their shadowy cote the white breasts peep
Of doves in a silver-feathered sleep;
A harvest mouse goes scampering by,
With silver claws, and silver eye;
And moveless fish in the water gleam,
By silver reeds in a silver stream.

Walter de la Mare

THE LISTENERS

" Is there anybody there ? " said the Traveller,
  Knocking on the moonlit door;
And his horse in the silence champed the grasses
  Of the forest's ferny floor;
And a bird flew up out of the turret,
  Above the Traveller's head:
And he smote upon the door again a second time;
  " Is there anybody there ? " he said.
But no one descended to the Traveller;
  No head from the leaf-fringed sill
Leaned over and looked into his grey eyes,
  Where he stood perplexed and still.
But only a host of phantom listeners
  That dwelt in the lone house then
Stood listening in the quiet of the moonlight
  To that voice from the world of men:
Stood thronging the faint moonbeams on the dark
    stair,
  That goes down to the empty hall,
Hearkening in an air stirred and shaken
  By the lonely Traveller's call.

And still would remain
    My wit to try—
My worn reeds broken,
    The dark tarn dry,
All words forgotten—
    Thou, Lord, and I.
                        Walter de la Mare

HAUNTED

THE rabbit in his burrow keeps
No guarded watch, in peace he sleeps;
The wolf that howls in challenging night
Cowers to her lair at morning light;
The simplest bird entwines a nest
Where she may lean her lovely breast,
Couched in the silence of the bough.
But thou, O man, what rest hast thou?

Thy emptiest solitude can bring
Only a subtler questioning
In thy divided heart. Thy bed
Recalls at dawn what midnight said.
Seek how thou wilt to feign content,
Thy flaming ardour is quickly spent;
Soon thy last company is gone,
And leaves thee—with thyself—alone.

Pomp and great friends may hem thee round,
A thousand busy tasks be found;
Earth's thronging beauties may beguile
Thy longing lovesick heart awhile;
And pride, like clouds of sunset, spread
A changing glory round thy head;
But fade will all; and thou must come,
Hating thy journey, homeless, home.

Rave how thou wilt; unmoved, remote,
That inward presence slumbers not,
Frets out each secret from thy breast,
Gives thee no rally, pause, nor rest,
Scans close thy very thoughts, lest they
Should sap his patient power away,
Answers thy wrath with peace, thy cry
With tenderest taciturnity.

Walter de la Mare

DREAMS

Be gentle, O hands of a child;
Be true: like a shadowy sea
In the starry darkness of night
    Are your eyes to me.

But words are shallow, and soon
Dreams fade that the heart once knew;
And youth fades out in the mind,
    In the dark eyes too.

What can a tired heart say,
Which the wise of the world have made dumb?
Save to the lonely dreams of a child,
    " Return again, come!"

Walter de la Mare

THE STRANGER

Half-hidden in a graveyard,
    In the blackness of a yew,
Where never living creature stirs,
    Nor sunbeam pierces through,

Sing such a history
   Of come and gone,
Their every drop is as wise
   As Solomon.

Very old are we men;
   Our dreams are tales
Told in dim Eden
   By Eve's nightingales;
We wake and whisper awhile,
   But, the day gone by,
Silence and sleep like fields
   Of amaranth lie.

Walter de la Mare

A BALLAD TO QUEEN ELIZABETH

(OF THE SPANISH ARMADA)

KING PHILIP had vaunted his claims;
   He had sworn for a year he would sack us;
With an army of heathenish names
   He was coming to fagot and stack us;
   Like the thieves of the sea he would track us,
And shatter our ships on the main;
   But we had bold Neptune to back us,—
And where are the galleons of Spain?

His carackes were christened of dames
   To the kirtles whereof he would tack us;
With his saints and his gilded stern-frames,
   He had thought like an egg-shell to crack us:
   Now Howard may get to his Flaccus,
And Drake to his Devon again,
   And Hawkins bowl rubbers to Bacchus,—
For where are the galleons of Spain?

Let his Majesty hang to St. James
   The axe that he whetted to hack us;
He must play at some lustier games
   Or at sea he can hope to out-thwack us;
   To his mines of Peru he would pack us
To tug at his bullet and chain;
   Alas! that his Greatness should lack us!—
But where are the galleons of Spain?

Envoy

   Gloriana! the Don may attack us
Whenever his stomach be fain;
   He must reach us before he can rack us,
And where are the galleons of Spain?

                  Austin Dobson

RUTH

" She stands breast high amid the corn "—
   The harvest of her love and tears
And every pain her soul has borne
   Through the fulfilling years.

She stoops amid the golden wealth
   That drops around her patient feet,
Gathering her suffering and her health—
   Her spirit's ripened wheat.

She gleans, unwearied, evermore
   The great ears of her joy and grief,
And binds the wonders of her store
   Into a little sheaf.

Bruising the grain of all she is,
   She kneads a little loaf of bread,

Mingling her life's strange mysteries—
    Loins, bosom, heart and head.

And then upon herself she feeds
    The life she loves, the lives she bears,
Breaking her passion for their needs,
    Her pity for their cares.

So, through her days' allotted span,
    She yields and binds and spends her truth ;
The woman GOD has given to man—
    The everlasting Ruth.

May Doney

THEY ARE NOT LONG

Vitæ summa brevis spem nos vetat incohare longam

THEY are not long, the weeping and the laughter,
    Love and desire and hate :
I think they have no portion in us after
    We pass the gate.

They are not long, the days of wine and roses :
    Out of a misty dream
Our path emerges for awhile, then closes
    Within a dream.

Ernest Dowson

THE CARTHUSIANS

THROUGH what long heaviness, assayed in what
    strange fire,
    Have these white monks been brought into the
    way of peace,
Despising the world's wisdom and the world's desire,
    Which from the body of this death brings no
    release ?

Within their austere walls no voices penetrate ;
  A sacred silence only, as of death, obtains ;
Nothing finds entry here of loud or passionate :
  This quiet is the exceeding profit of their pains.

From many lands they came, in divers fiery ways ;
  Each knew at last the vanity of earthly joys ;
And one was crowned with thorns, and one was
    crowned with bays,
  And each was tired at last of the world's foolish
    noise.

It was not theirs with Dominic to preach God's
    holy wrath,
  They were too stern to bear sweet Francis' gentle
    sway ;
Theirs was a higher calling and a steeper path,
  To dwell alone with Christ, to meditate and pray.

A cloistered company, they are companionless,
  None knoweth here the secret of his brother's
    heart :
They are but come together for more loneliness,
  Whose bond is solitude and silence all their part.

O beatific life ! Who is there shall gainsay
  Your great refusal's victory, your little loss,
Deserting vanity for the more perfect way,
  The sweeter service of the most dolorous Cross ?

Ye shall prevail at last ! Surely ye shall prevail !
  Your silence and austerity shall win at last :
Desire and mirth, the world's ephemeral lights shall
    fail,
  The sweet star of your queen is never overcast.

We fling up flowers and laugh, we laugh across the
　　wine ;
　　With wine we dull our souls and careful strains
　　　of art ;
Our cups are polished skulls round which the roses
　　twine :
　　None dares to look at Death who leers and lurks
　　　apart.

Move on, white company, whom that has not
　　sufficed !
　　Our viols cease, our wine is death, our roses fail :
Pray for our heedlessness, O dwellers with the
　　Christ !
　　Though the world fall apart, surely ye shall
　　　prevail.

Ernest Dowson

THE MIDLANDS

BLACK in the summer night my Cotswold hill
　　Aslant my window sleeps, beneath a sky
Deep as the bedded violets that fill
　　March woods with dusky passion. As I lie
Abed between cool walls I watch the host
　　Of the slow stars lit over Gloucester plain,
And drowsily the habit of these most
　　Beloved of English lands moves in my brain,
While silence holds dominion of the dark,
Save when the foxes from the spinneys bark.

I see the valleys in their morning mist
　　Wreathed under limpid hills in moving light,
Happy with many a yeoman melodist :
　　I see the little roads of twinkling white

Busy with fieldward teams and market gear
  Of rosy men, cloth-gaitered, who can tell
The many-minded changes of the year,
  Who know why crops and kine fare ill or well;
I see the sun persuade the mist away,
Till town and stead are shining to the day.

I see the wagons move along the rows
  Of ripe and summer-breathing clover-flower,
I see the lissom husbandman who knows
  Deep in his heart the beauty of his power,
As, lithely pitched, the full-heaped fork bids on
  The harvest home. I hear the rickyard fill
With gossip as in generations gone,
  While wagon follows wagon from the hill.
I think how, when our seasons all are sealed,
Shall come the unchanging harvest from the field.

I see the barns and comely manors planned
  By men who somehow moved in comely thought,
Who, with a simple shippon to their hand,
  As men upon some godlike business wrought;
I see the little cottages that keep
  Their beauty still where since Plantagenet
Have come the shepherds happily to sleep,
  Finding the loaves and cups of cider set;
I see the twisted shepherds, brown and old,
Driving at dusk their glimmering sheep to fold.

And now the valleys that upon the sun
  Broke from their opal veils are veiled again,
And the last light upon the wolds is done,
  And silence falls on flocks and fields and men;
And black upon the night I watch my hill,
  And the stars shine, and there an owly wing

Brushes the night, and all again is still,
   And, from this land of worship that I sing,
I turn to sleep, content that from my sires
I draw the blood of England's midmost shires.

John Drinkwater

OF GREATHAM

FOR peace, than knowledge more desirable,
   Into your Sussex quietness I came,
When summer's green and gold and azure fell
   Over the world in flame.

And peace upon your pasture-lands I found,
   Where grazing flocks drift on continually,
As little clouds that travel with no sound
   Across a windless sky.

Out of your oaks the birds call to their mates
   That brood among the pines, where hidden deep
From curious eyes a world's adventure waits
   In columned choirs of sleep.

Under the calm ascension of the night
   We heard the mellow lapsing and return
Of night-owls purring in their groundling flight
   Through lanes of darkling fern.

Unbroken peace when all the stars were drawn
   Back to their lairs of light, and ranked along
From shire to shire the downs out of the dawn
   Were risen in golden song.

.   .   .   .   .   .

I sing of peace who have known the large unrest
  Of men bewildered in their travelling,
And I have known the bridal earth unblest
  By the brigades of spring.

I have known that loss. And now the broken
      thought
  Of nations marketing in death I know,
The very winds to threnodies are wrought
  That on your downlands blow.

I sing of peace. Was it but yesterday
  I came among your roses and your corn ?
Then momently amid this wrath I pray
  For yesterday reborn.

                              John Drinkwater

AN AFTERTHOUGHT ON APPLES

WHILE yet unfallen apples throng the bough,
To ripen as they cling
In lieu of the lost bloom, I ponder how
Myself did flower in so rough a spring,
And was not set in grace
When the first flush was gone from summer's face.
How in my tardy season, making one
Of a crude congregation, sour in sin,
I nodded like a green-clad mandarin,
Averse from all that savoured of the sun.
  But now throughout these last autumnal weeks
What skyey gales mine arrogant station thresh,
What sunbeams mellow my beshadowed cheeks,
What steely storms cudgel mine obdurate flesh ;
Less loth am I to see my fellows launch

Forth from my side into the air's abyss,
Whose own stalk is
Grown untenacious of its wonted branch.
  And yet, O God,
Tumble me not at last upon the sod,
Or, still superb above my fallen kind,
Grant not my golden rind
To the black starlings screaming in the mist.
Nay, rather on some gentle day and bland
Give Thou Thyself my stalk a little twist,
Dear Lord, and I shall fall into Thy hand.

Helen Parry Eden

LA FIGLIA CHE PIANGE

O quam te memorem virgo . . . O dea certe !

STAND on the highest pavement of the stair—
Lean on a garden urn—
Weave, weave the sunlight in your hair—
Clasp your flowers to you with a pained surprise—
Fling them to the ground and turn
With a fugitive resentment in your eyes:
But weave, weave the sunlight in your hair.

So I would have had him leave,
So I would have had her stand and grieve,
So he would have left
As the soul leaves the body torn and bruised,
As the mind deserts the body it has used.
I should find
Some way incomparably light and deft,
Some way we both should understand,
Simple and faithless as a smile and shake of the
    hand.

She turned away, but with the autumn weather
Compelled my imagination many days,
Many days and many hours:
Her hair over her arms and her arms full of flowers.
And I wonder how they should have been together!
I should have lost a gesture and a pose.
Sometimes these cogitations still amaze
The troubled midnight and the noon's repose.

T. S. Eliot

A SHIP, AN ISLE, A SICKLE MOON

A SHIP, an isle, a sickle moon—
With few but with how splendid stars
The mirrors of the sea are strewn
Between their silver bars!

.   .   .   .   .

An isle beside an isle she lay,
The pale ship anchored in the bay,
While in the young moon's port of gold
A star-ship—as the mirrors told—
Put forth its great and lonely light
To the unreflecting Ocean, Night.
And still, a ship upon her seas,
The isle and the island cypresses
Went sailing on without the gale:
And still there moved the moon so pale,
A crescent ship without a sail!

James Elroy Flecker

TO A POET A THOUSAND YEARS HENCE

I who am dead a thousand years,
   And wrote this sweet archaic song,
Send you my words for messengers
   The way I shall not pass along.

I care not if you bridge the seas,
   Or ride secure the cruel sky,
Or build consummate palaces
   Of metal or of masonry.

But have you wine and music still,
   And statues and a bright-eyed love,
And foolish thoughts of good and ill,
   And prayers to them who sit above?

How shall we conquer? Like a wind
   That falls at eve our fancies blow,
And old Mæonides the blind
   Said it three thousand years ago.

O friend unseen, unborn, unknown,
   Student of our sweet English tongue,
Read out my words at night, alone:
   I was a poet, I was young.

Since I can never see your face,
   And never shake you by the hand,
I send my soul through time and space
   To greet you. You will understand.

James Elroy Flecker

THE OLD SHIPS

I HAVE seen old ships sail like swans asleep
Beyond the village which men still call Tyre,
With leaden age o'ercargoed, dipping deep
For Famagusta and the hidden sun
That rings black Cyprus with a lake of fire;
And all those ships were certainly so old—
Who knows how oft with squat and noisy gun,
Questing brown slaves or Syrian oranges,
The pirate Genoese
Hell-raked them till they rolled
Blood, water, fruit and corpses up the hold?
But now through friendly seas they softly run,
Painted the mid-sea blue or the shore-sea green,
Still patterned with the vine and grapes in gold.

But I have seen,
Pointing her shapely shadows from the dawn
And image tumbled on a rose-swept bay,
A drowsy ship of some yet older day;
And, wonder's breath indrawn,
Thought I—who knows—who knows—but in that
    same
(Fished up beyond Aeaea, patched up new
—Stern painted brighter blue—)
That talkative, bald-headed seaman came
(Twelve patient comrades sweating at the oar)
From Troy's doom-crimson shore,
And with great lies about his wooden horse
Set the crew laughing, and forgot his course?

It was so old a ship—who knows, who knows?
—And yet so beautiful, I watched in vain
To see the mast burst open with a rose,
And the whole deck put on its leaves again.

James Elroy Flecker

TENEBRIS INTERLUCENTEM

A LINNET who had lost her way
   Sang on a blackened bough in Hell,
   Till all the ghosts remembered well
The trees, the wind, the golden day.

At last they knew that they had died
   When they heard music in that land,
   And some one there stole forth a hand
To draw a brother to his side.

James Elroy Flecker

THE DYING PATRIOT

DAY breaks on England down the Kentish hills,
Singing in the silence of the meadow-footing rills,
   Day of my dreams, O day!
  I saw them march from Dover, long ago,
   With a silver cross before them, singing low,
Monks of Rome from their home where the blue
     seas break in foam,
   Augustine with his feet of snow.

Noon strikes on England, noon on Oxford town,
—Beauty she was statue cold—there's blood upon
   her gown:

Noon of my dreams, O noon!
  Proud and godly kings had built her, long ago,
  With her towers and tombs and statues all arow,
With her fair and floral air and the love that
    lingers there,
  And the streets where the great men go.

Evening on the olden, the golden sea of Wales,
When the first star shivers and the last wave pales:
O evening dreams!
  There's a house that Britons walked in, long ago,
  Where now the springs of ocean fall and flow,
And the dead robed in red and sea-lilies overhead
  Sway when the long winds blow.

Sleep not, my country: though night is here, afar
Your children of the morning are clamorous for
    war:
Fire in the night, O dreams!
  Though she send you as she sent you, long ago,
  South to desert, east to ocean, west to snow,
West of these out to seas colder than the Hebrides
    I must go
Where the fleet of stars is anchored and the young
    Star-captains glow.

James Elroy Flecker

THE EVENING SKY

ROSE-BOSOM'D and rose-limb'd,
With eyes of dazzling bright
Shakes Venus mid the twined boughs of the night;
Rose-limb'd, soft-stepping

IT WAS THE LOVELY MOON

It was the lovely moon—she lifted
Slowly her white brow among
Bronze cloud-waves that ebbed and drifted
Faintly, faintlier afar.
Calm she looked, yet pale with wonder,
Sweet in unwonted thoughtfulness,
Watching the earth that dwindled under
Faintly, faintlier afar.
It was the lovely moon that lovelike
Hovered over the wandering, tired
Earth, her bosom grey and dovelike,
Hovering beautiful as a dove. . . .
The lovely moon :—her soft light falling
Lightly on roof and poplar and pine—
Tree to tree whispering and calling,
Wonderful in the silvery shine
Of the round, lovely, thoughtful moon.

John Freeman

MUSIC COMES

Music comes
Sweetly from the trembling string
When wizard fingers sweep
Dreamily, half asleep ;
When through remembering reeds
Ancient airs and murmurs creep,
Oboe oboe following,
Flute answering clear high flute,
Voices, voices—falling mute,
And the jarring drums.

At night I heard
First a waking bird
Out of the quiet darkness sing . . .
Music comes
Strangely to the brain asleep!
And I heard
Soft, wizard fingers sweep
Music from the trembling string,
And through remembering reeds
Ancient airs and murmurs creep;
Oboe oboe following,
Flute calling clear high flute,
Voices faint, falling mute,
And low jarring drums;
Then all those airs
Sweetly jangled—newly strange,
Rich with change . . .
Was it the wind in the reeds?
Did the wind range
Over the trembling string;
Into flute and oboe pouring
Solemn music; sinking, soaring
Low to high,
Up and down the sky?
Was it the wind jarring
Drowsy far-off drums?

Strangely to the brain asleep
Music comes.

                                    John Freeman

IN THAT DARK SILENT HOUR

In that dark silent hour
When the wind wants power,
And in the black height
The sky wants light,
Stirless and black
In utter lack,
And not a sound
Escapes from that untroubled round :—

To wake then
In the dark, and ache then
Until the dark is gone—
Lonely, yet not alone ;
Hearing another's breath
All the quiet beneath,
Knowing one sleeps near
That day held dear

And dreams held dear ; but now
In this sharp moment—how
Share the moment's sweetness,
Forego its completeness,
Nor be alone
Now the dark is grown
Spiritual and deep
More than in dreams and sleep ?

O, it is pain, 'tis need
That so will plead
For a little loneliness.
If it be pain to miss
Loved touch, look and lip,
Companionship
Yet is verier pain
Then, then

In that dark silent hour
When the wind wants power,
And you, near or far, sleep,
And your released thoughts towards me creep,
While I, imprisoned, awake,
Ache—ache
To be for one
Long, little moment with myself alone.

John Freeman

FAIRY MUSIC

WHEN the fiddlers play their tunes you may some-
    times hear,
Very softly chiming in, magically clear,
Magically high and sweet, the tiny crystal notes
Of fairy voices bubbling free from tiny fairy throats.

When the birds at break of day chant their morning
    prayers,
Or on sunny afternoons pipe ecstatic airs,
Comes an added rush of sound to the silver din—
Songs of fairy troubadours gaily joining in.

When athwart the drowsy fields summer twilight
    falls,
Through the tranquil air there float elfin madrigals,
And in wild November nights, on the winds astride,
Fairy hosts go rushing by, singing as they ride.

Every dream that mortals dream, sleeping or awake,
Every lovely fragile hope—these the fairies take,
Delicately fashion them and give them back again
In tender, limpid melodies that charm the hearts
    of men.

Rose Fyleman

FLANNAN ISLE

THOUGH three men dwell on Flannan Isle
To keep the lamp alight,
As we steer'd under the lee we caught
No glimmer through the night!

A passing ship at dawn had brought
The news, and quickly we set sail
To find out what strange thing might ail
The keepers of the deep-sea light.

The winter day broke blue and bright,
With glancing sun and glancing spray,
As o'er the swell our boat made way,
As gallant as a gull in flight.

But, as we neared the lonely Isle
And look'd up at the naked height,
And saw the lighthouse towering white
With blinded lantern that all night
Had never shot a spark
Of comfort through the dark,
So ghostly in the cold sunlight
It seem'd, that we were struck the while
With wonder all too dread for words.
And, as into the tiny creek
We stole, beneath the hanging crag
We saw three queer, black, ugly birds—
Too big by far, in my belief,
For guillemot or shag—
Like seamen sitting bolt-upright
Upon a half-tide reef:
But as we neared they plunged from sight
Without a sound or spurt of white.

And still too mazed to speak,
We landed and made fast the boat
And climbed the track in single file,
Each wishing he was safe afloat
On any sea, however far,
So it be far from Flannan Isle :
And still we seemed to climb, and climb
As though we'd lost all count of time
And so must climb for evermore ;
Yet, all too soon, we reached the door—
The black, sun-blister'd lighthouse-door
That gaped for us ajar.

As on the threshold for a spell
We paused, we seem'd to breathe the smell
Of limewash and of tar,
Familiar as our daily breath,
As though 'twere some strange scent of death ;
And so, yet wondering, side by side,
We stood a moment, still tongue-tied,
And each with black foreboding eyed
The door ere we should fling it wide
To leave the sunlight for the gloom :
Till, plucking courage up, at last,
Hard on each other's heels we passed
Into the living-room.

Yet as we crowded through the door
We only saw a table spread
For dinner, meat and cheese and bread,
But all untouched, and no one there :
As though, when they sat down to eat,
Ere they could even taste,
Alarm had come and they in haste
Had risen and left the bread and meat,

Until I stumbled unawares
Upon a creek where big white bears
Plunged headlong down with flourished heels
And floundered after shining seals
Through shivering seas of blinding blue.
And, as I watched them, ere I knew,
I'd stripped and I was swimming, too,
Among the seal-pack, young and hale,
And thrusting on with threshing tail,
With twist and twirl and sudden leap
Through crackling ice and salty deep,
Diving and doubling with my kind
Until at last we left behind
Those big white blundering bulks of death,
And lay at length with panting breath
Upon a far untravelled floe,
Beneath a gentle drift of snow—
Snow drifting gently, fine and white
Out of the endless Polar night,
Falling and falling evermore
Upon that far untravelled shore
Till I was buried fathoms deep
Beneath that cold white drifting sleep—
Sleep drifting deep,
Deep drifting sleep. . . .

The carter cracked a sudden whip:
I clutched my stool with startled grip,
Awakening to the grimy heat
Of that intolerable street.

Wilfrid Wilson Gibson

LAMENT

WE who are left, how shall we look again
Happily on the sun or feel the rain,
Without remembering how they who went
Ungrudgingly, and spent
Their lives for us, loved too the sun and the rain?

A bird among the rain-wet lilac sings—
But we, how shall we turn to little things
And listen to the birds and winds and streams
Made holy by their dreams,
Nor feel the heart-break in the heart of things?

Wilfrid Wilson Gibson

THE CHARCOAL-BURNER

HE lives within the hollow wood,
  From one clear dell he seldom ranges;
His daily toil in solitude
  Revolves, but never changes.

A still old man, with grizzled beard,
  Grey eye, bent shape, and smoke-tanned features,
His quiet footstep is not feared
  By shyest woodland creatures.

I love to watch the pale blue spire
  His scented labour builds above it;
I track the woodland by his fire,
  And, seen afar, I love it.

Yonder the long horizon lies, and there by night
    and day
The old ships draw to home again, the young
    ships sail away;
And come I may, but go I must, and, if men ask
    you why,
You may put the blame on the stars and the Sun
    and the white road and the sky.

Gerald Gould

THE HAPPY TREE

THERE was a bright and happy tree;
    The wind with music laced its boughs:
Thither across the houseless sea
    Came singing birds to house.

Men grudged the tree its happy eves,
    Its happy dawns of eager sound;
So all that crown and tower of leaves
    They levelled with the ground.

They made an upright of the stem,
    A cross-piece of a bough they made:
No shadow of their deed on them
    The fallen branches laid.

But blithely, since the year was young,
    When they a fitting hill did find,
There on the happy tree they hung
    The Saviour of mankind.

Gerald Gould

STAR-TALK

" ARE you awake, Gemelli,
    This frosty night ? "
" We'll be awake till reveillé,
Which is Sunrise," say the Gemelli,
" It's no good trying to go to sleep :
If there's wine to be got we'll drink it deep,
    But rest is hopeless to-night,
    But rest is hopeless to-night."

" Are you cold too, poor Pleiads,
    This frosty night ? "
" Yes, and so are the Hyads :
See us cuddle and hug," say the Pleiads,
" All six in a ring : it keeps us warm :
We huddle together like birds in a storm :
    It's bitter weather to-night,
    It's bitter weather to-night."

" What do you hunt, Orion,
    This starry night ? "
" The Ram, the Bull and the Lion,
And the Great Bear," says Orion,
" With my starry quiver and beautiful belt
I am trying to find a good thick pelt
    To warm my shoulders to-night,
    To warm my shoulders to-night."

" Did you hear that, Great She-bear,
    This frosty night ? "
" Yes, he's talking of stripping *me* bare
Of my own big fur," says the She-bear.

All the bright company of heaven
  Hold him in their high comradeship,
The Dog-Star and the Sisters Seven,
  Orion's Belt and sworded hip.

The woodland trees that stand together,
  They stand to him each one a friend;
They gently speak in the windy weather;
  They guide to valley and ridge's end.

The kestrel hovering by day,
  And the little owls that call by night,
Bid him be swift and keen as they,
  As keen of ear, as swift of sight.

The blackbird sings to him, "Brother, brother,
  If this be the last song you shall sing,
Sing well, for you may not sing another;
  Brother, sing."

In dreary, doubtful, waiting hours,
  Before the brazen frenzy starts,
The horses show him nobler powers;
  O patient eyes, courageous hearts!

And when the burning moment breaks,
  And all things else are out of mind,
And only joy of battle takes
  Him by the throat, and makes him blind,

Through joy and blindness he shall know,
  Not caring much to know, that still
Nor lead nor steel shall reach him, so
  That it be not the Destined Will.

The thundering line of battle stands,
  And in the air Death moans and sings;
But Day shall clasp him with strong hands,
  And night shall fold him in soft wings.

Julian Grenfell

WHEN I SET OUT FOR LYONNESSE

WHEN I set out for Lyonnesse,
  A hundred miles away,
  The rime was on the spray,
And starlight lit my lonesomeness
When I set out for Lyonnesse
  A hundred miles away.

What would bechance at Lyonnesse
  While I should sojourn there
  No prophet durst declare,
Nor did the wisest wizard guess
What would bechance at Lyonnesse
  While I should sojourn there.

When I came back from Lyonnesse
  With magic in my eyes,
  All marked with mute surmise
My radiance rare and fathomless,
When I came back from Lyonnesse
  With magic in my eyes.

Thomas Hardy

BEENY CLIFF
March 1870–*March* 1913

I

O THE opal and the sapphire of that wandering
  western sea,
And the woman riding high above with bright
  hair flapping free—
The woman whom I loved so, and who loyally
  loved me.

II

The pale mews plained below us, and the waves
  seemed far away
In a nether sky, engrossed in saying their cease-
  less babbling say,
As we laughed light-heartedly aloft on that clear-
  sunned March day.

III

A little cloud then cloaked us, and there flew an
  irised rain,
And the Atlantic dyed its levels with a dull mis-
  featured stain,
And then the sun burst out again, and purples
  prinked the main.

IV

—Still in all its chasmal beauty bulks old Beeny
  to the sky.
And shall she and I not go there once again now
  March is nigh,
And the sweet things said in that March say anew
  there by and by?

v

What if still in chasmal beauty looms that wild
    weird western shore?
The woman now is—elsewhere—whom the ambling
    pony bore,
And nor knows nor cares for Beeny, and will laugh
    there nevermore.

Thomas Hardy

THE SOULS OF THE SLAIN

I

THE thick lids of Night closed upon me
        Alone at the Bill
        Of the Isle by the Race *—
    Many-caverned, bald, wrinkled of face—
And with darkness and silence the spirit was on me
        To brood and be still.

II

No wind fanned the flats of the ocean,
        Or promontory sides,
        Or the ooze by the strand,
    Or the bent-bearded slope of the land,
Whose base took its rest amid everlong motion
        Of criss-crossing tides.

III

Soon from out of the Southward seemed nearing
        A whirr, as of wings
        Waved by mighty-vanned flies,
    Or by night-moths of measureless size,
And in softness and smoothness well-nigh beyond
        hearing
        Of corporal things.

* The "Race" is the turbulent sea-area off the Bill of Port-
land, where contrary tides meet.

IV

And they bore to the bluff, and alighted—
       A dim-discerned train
       Of sprites without mould,
Frameless souls none might touch or might hold—
On the ledge by the turreted lantern, far-sighted
       By men of the main.

V

And I heard them say " Home ! " and I knew them
       For souls of the felled
       On the earth's nether bord
Under Capricorn, whither they'd warred,
And I neared in my awe, and gave heedfulness to
       them
       With breathings inheld.

VI

Then, it seemed, there approached from the north
       ward
       A senior soul-flame
       Of the like filmy hue :
And he met them and spake : " Is it you,
O my men ? " Said they, " Aye ! We bear home-
       ward and hearthward
       To feast on our fame ! "

VII

" I've flown there before you," he said then :
       " Your households are well :
       But—your kin linger less
On your glory and war-mightiness
Than on dearer things."—" Dearer ? " cried these
       from the dead then,
       " Of what do they tell ? "

VIII

" Some mothers muse sadly, and murmur
    Your doings as boys—
    Recall the quaint ways
Of your babyhood's innocent days.
Some pray that, ere dying, your faith had grown
    firmer,
    And higher your joys.

IX

" A father broods : ' Would I had set him
    To some humble trade,
    And so slacked his high fire,
And his passionate martial desire ;
Had told him no stories to woo him and whet him
    To this dire crusade ! ' "

X

" And, General, how hold out our sweethearts,
    Sworn loyal as doves ? "
    —" Many mourn ; many think
It is not unattractive to prink
Them in sables for heroes. Some fickle and fleet
    hearts
    Have found them new loves."

XI

" And our wives ? " quoth another resignedly,
    " Dwell they on our deeds ? "
    —" Deeds of home ; that live yet
Fresh as new—deeds of fondness or fret ;
Ancient words that were kindly expressed or
    unkindly,
    These, these have their heeds."

XII

—" Alas ! then it seems that our glory
　　Weighs less in their thought
　　Than our old homely acts,
　And the long-ago commonplace facts
Of our lives—held by us as scarce part of our story,
　　And rated as nought ! "

XIII

Then bitterly some : " Was it wise now
　　To raise the tomb-door
　　For such knowledge ?　Away ! "
　But the rest : " Fame we prized till to-day ;
Yet that hearts keep us green for old kindness we
　　prize now
　　A thousand times more ! "

XIV

Thus speaking, the trooped apparitions
　　Began to disband
　　And resolve them in two ;
　Those whose record was lovely and true
Bore to northward for home : those of bitter
　　traditions
　　Again left the land,

XV

And, towering to seaward in legions,
　　They paused at a spot
　　Overbending the Race—
　That engulphing, ghast, sinister place—
Whither headlong they plunged to the fathomless
　　regions
　　Of myriads forgot.

xvi

And the spirits of those who were homing
        Passed on, rushingly,
        Like the Pentecost Wind;
    And the whirr of their wayfaring thinned
And surceased on the sky, and but left in the
        gloaming
            Sea-mutterings and me.

Thomas Hardy

December, 1899

THE OXEN

Christmas Eve, and twelve of the clock.
    " Now they are all on their knees,"
An elder said as we sat in a flock
    By the embers in hearthside ease.

We pictured the meek mild creatures where
    They dwelt in their strawy pen,
Nor did it occur to one of us there
    To doubt they were kneeling then.

So fair a fancy few would weave
    In these years ! Yet, I feel,
If some one said on Christmas Eve,
    " Come ; see the oxen kneel

" In the lonely barton by yonder coomb
    Our childhood used to know,"
I should go with him in the gloom,
    Hoping it might be so.

Thomas Hardy

IN TIME OF " THE BREAKING OF NATIONS "

I

ONLY a man harrowing clods
  In a slow silent walk
With an old horse that stumbles and nods
  Half asleep as they stalk.

II

Only thin smoke without flame
  From the heaps of couch-grass ;
Yet this will go onward the same
  Though Dynasties pass.

III

Yonder a maid and her wight
  Come whispering by :
War's annals will cloud into night
  Ere their story die.

Thomas Hardy

BEYOND THE LAST LAMP

(NEAR TOOTING COMMON)

I

WHILE rain, with eve in partnership,
Descended darkly, drip, drip, drip,
Beyond the last lone lamp I passed
  Walking slowly, whispering sadly,
  Two linked loiterers, wan, downcast :
Some heavy thought constrained each face,
And blinded them to time and place.

II

The pair seemed lovers, yet absorbed
In mental scenes no longer orbed
By love's young rays. Each countenance
   As it slowly, as it sadly
   Caught the lamplight's yellow glance,
Held in suspense a misery
At things which had been or might be.

III

When I retrod that watery way
Some hours beyond the droop of day,
Still I found pacing there the twain
   Just as slowly, just as sadly,
   Heedless of the night and rain.
One could but wonder who they were,
And what wild woe detained them there.

IV

Though thirty years of blur and blot
Have slid since I beheld that spot,
And saw in curious converse there
   Moving slowly, moving sadly,
   That mysterious tragic pair,
Its olden look may linger on—
All but the couple ; they have gone.

V

Whither ? Who knows, indeed ? . . . And **yet**
To me, when nights are weird and wet,

The smoke ascends
In a rosy-and-golden haze. The spires
Shine, and are changed. In the valley
Shadows rise. The lark sings on. The sun,
Closing his benediction,
Sinks, and the darkening air
Thrills with a sense of the triumphing night—
Night with her train of stars
And her great gift of sleep.

So be my passing!
My task accomplish'd and the long day done,
My wages taken, and in my heart
Some late lark singing,
Let me be gathered to the quiet west,
The sundown splendid and serene,
Death.

William Ernest Henley

UNCONQUERABLE

OUT of the night that covers me,
    Black as the pit from pole to pole,
I thank whatever gods may be
    For my unconquerable soul.

In the fell clutch of circumstance
    I have not winced nor cried aloud.
Under the bludgeonings of chance
    My head is bloody, but unbow'd.

Beyond this place of wrath and tears
    Looms but the Horror of the shade,
And yet the menace of the years
    Finds, and shall find, me unafraid.

It matters not how strait the gate,
  How charged with punishments the scroll,
I am the master of my fate:
  I am the captain of my soul.

William Ernest Henley

THE BELLS OF HEAVEN

'Twould ring the bells of Heaven
The wildest peal for years,
If Parson lost his senses
And people came to theirs,
And he and they together
Knelt down with angry prayers
For tamed and shabby tigers
And dancing dogs and bears,
And wretched, blind pit ponies,
And little hunted hares.

Ralph Hodgson

STUPIDITY STREET

I saw with open eyes
  Singing birds sweet
Sold in the shops
  For the people to eat,
Sold in the shops of
  Stupidity Street.

I saw in vision
  The worm in the wheat,
And in the shops nothing
  For people to eat;
Nothing for sale in
  Stupidity Street.

Ralph Hodgson

Standing with his head hung down
In a stupor, dreaming things :
Green savannas, jungles brown,
Battlefields and bellowings,
Bulls undone and lions dead
And vultures flapping overhead.

Dreaming things : of days he spent
With his mother gaunt and lean
In the valley warm and green,
Full of baby wonderment,
Blinking out of silly eyes
At a hundred mysteries ;

Dreaming over once again
How he wandered with a throng
Of bulls and cows a thousand strong,
Wandered on from plain to plain,
Up the hill and down the dale,
Always at his mother's tail ;

How he lagged behind the herd,
Lagged and tottered, weak of limb,
And she turned and ran to him
Blaring at the loathly bird
Stationed always in the skies,
Waiting for the flesh that dies.

Dreaming maybe of a day
When her drained and drying paps
Turned him to the sweets and saps,
Richer fountains by the way,
And she left the bull she bore,
And he looked to her no more ;

And his little frame grew stout,
And his little legs grew strong,
And the way was not so long;
And his little horns came out,
And he played at butting trees
And boulder-stones and tortoises,

Joined a game of knobby skulls
With the youngsters of his year,
All the other little bulls,
Learning both to bruise and bear,
Learning how to stand a shock
Like a little bull of rock.

Dreaming of a day less dim,
Dreaming of a time less far,
When the faint but certain star
Of destiny burned clear for him,
And a fierce and wild unrest
Broke the quiet of his breast,

And the gristles of his youth
Hardened in his comely pow,
And he came to fighting growth,
Beat his bull and won his cow,
And flew his tail and trampled off
Past the tallest, vain enough,

And curved about in splendour full,
And curved again and snuffed the airs
As who should say Come out who dares!
And all beheld a bull, a Bull,
And knew that here was surely one
That backed for no bull, fearing none.
8

And the leader of the herd
Looked and saw, and beat the ground,
And shook the forest with his sound,
Bellowed at the loathly bird
Stationed always in the skies
Waiting for the flesh that dies.

Dreaming, this old bull forlorn,
Surely dreaming of the hour
When he came to sultan power,
And they owned him master-horn,
Chiefest bull of all among
Bulls and cows a thousand strong;

And in all the tramping herd
Not a bull that barred his way,
Not a cow that said him nay,
Not a bull or cow that erred
In the furnace of his look
Dared a second, worse rebuke;

Not in all the forest wide,
Jungle, thicket, pasture, fen,
Not another dared him then,
Dared him and again defied;
Not a sovereign buck or boar
Came a second time for more;

Not a serpent that survived
Once the terrors of his hoof
Risked a second time reproof,
Came a second time and lived,
Not a serpent in its skin
Came again for discipline;

Not a leopard bright as flame,
Flashing fingerhooks of steel
That a wooden tree might feel,
Met his fury once and came
For a second reprimand,
Not a leopard in the land.

Not a lion of them all,
Not a lion of the hills,
Hero of a thousand kills,
Dared a second fight and fall,
Dared that ram terrific twice,
Paid a second time the price.

Pity him, this dupe of dream,
Leader of the herd again
Only in his daft old brain,
Once again the bull supreme
And bull enough to bear the part
Only in his tameless heart.

Pity him that he must wake;
Even now the swarm of flies
Blackening his bloodshot eyes
Bursts and blusters round the lake,
Scattered from the feast half-fed,
By great shadows overhead;

And the dreamer turns away
From his visionary herds
And his splendid yesterday,
Turns to meet the loathly birds
Flocking round him from the skies,
Waiting for the flesh that dies.

Ralph Hodgson

I HAVE DESIRED TO GO

I HAVE desired to go
Where springs not fail,
To fields where flies no sharp and sided hail,
And a few lilies blow.

And I have asked to be
Where no storms come,
Where the green swell is in the havens dumb,
And out of the swing of the sea.

Gerard Manley Hopkins

THE OLD WAY

THERE'S a sea that lies uncharted far beyond the setting sun,
And a gallant Fleet was sailing there whose fighting days are done,
Sloop and Galleon, Brig and Pinnace, all the rigs you never met,
Fighting Frigate, grave Three-decker, with their snowy canvas set;
Dozed and dreamed, when, on a sudden, ev'ry sail began to swell,
For the breeze has spoken strangers, with a stirring tale to tell,
And a thousand eager voices flung the challenge out to sea:
" Come they hither in the old way, in the only way that's free ? "

And the flying Breeze called softly : " In the old
    way,
Through the winters and the waters of the North,
They have waited, ah the waiting, in the old way,
Strong and patient, from the Pentlands to the
    Forth.
There was fog to blind and baffle off the headlands,
There were gales to beat the worst that ever blew,
But they took it, as they found it, in the old way,
And I know it often helped to think of you."

'Twas a Frigate, under stun-sails, as she gently
    gathered way
Spoke in jerks, like all the Frigates, who have little
    time to stay :
" We'd to hurry, under Nelson, thank my timbers
    I was tough,
For he worked us as he loved us, and he never had
    enough.
Are the English mad as ever ? were the Frigates
    just as few ?
(Will their sheets be always stranding, ere the
    rigging's rove anew ?)
Just as Saxon slow at starting, just as weirdly
    wont to win ?
Had they Frigates out and watching ? Did they
    pass the signals in ? "

And the laughing Breeze made answer : " In
    the old way ;
You should see the little cruisers spread and fly,
Peering over the horizon, in the old way,
And a seaplane up and wheeling in the sky.
When the wireless snapped ' The enemy is sighted,'

If his accents were comparatively new,
Why, the sailor men were cheering, in the old way,
So I naturally smiled and thought of you."

Then a courtly voice and stately from a tall Three-
    decker came—
She'd the manners of a monarch and a story in
    her name ;
" We'd a winter gale at even, and my shrouds are
    aching yet,
It was more than time for reefing when the upper
    sails were set.
So we chased in woful weather, till we closed in
    failing light,
Then we fought them, as we caught them, just as
    Hawke had bid us fight ;
And we swept the sea by sunrise, clear and free
    beyond a doubt.
Was it thus the matter ended when the enemy was
    out ? "

  Cried the Breeze : " They fought and followed
      in the old way,
  For they raced to make a record all the while
  With a knot to veer and haul on, in the old way,
  That had never even met the measured mile—
  And the guns were making merry in the twilight,
  That the enemy was victor may be true,
  Still—he hurried into harbour—in the old way—
  And I wondered if he'd ever heard of you."

Came a gruff and choking chuckle, and a craft as
    black as doom
Lumbered laughing down to leeward, as the braves
    gave her room.

" Set 'un blazin', good your Lordships, for the tide
        be makin' strong,
Proper breeze to fan a fireship, set 'un drivin' out
        along !
Tis the ' Torch,' wi' humble duty, from Lord
        Howard 'board the ' Ark,'
We'm a laughin'-stock to Brixham, but a terror
        after dark,
Hold an' bilge anigh to burstin', pitch and sulphur,
        tar an' all,
Was it so, my dear, they'm fashioned for my Lord
        High Admiral ? "

    Cried the Breeze : " You'd hardly know it from
            the old way,
    (Gloriana, did you waken at the fight ?)
    Stricken shadows, scared and flying in the old way
    From the swift destroying spectres of the night,
    There were some that steamed and scattered
            south for safety,
    From the mocking western echo ' Where be tu ? '
    There were some that—got the message—in the
            old way,
    And the flashes in the darkness spoke of you."

There's a wondrous Golden Harbour, far beyond
        the setting sun,
Where a gallant ship may anchor when her fighting
        days are done,
Free from tempest, rock and battle, toil and tumult
        safely o'er,
Where the breezes murmur softly and there's peace
        for evermore.
They have climbed the last horizon, they are
        standing in from sea,

And the Pilot makes the Haven where a ship is
    glad to be :
Comes at last the glorious greeting, strangely new
    and ages old,
See the sober grey is shining like the Tudor green
    and gold !

And the waiting jibs are hoisted, in the old way,
As the guns begin to thunder down the line ;
Hear the silver trumpets calling, in the old way ꜟ
Over all the silken pennons float and shine.
" Did you voyage all unspoken, small and lonely ?
Or with fame, the happy fortune of the few ?
So you win the Golden Harbour, in the old way,
There's the old sea welcome waiting there for
    you."

R. A. Hopwood

THE PORTRAIT

SHE sits upon a tombstone in the shade ;
One flake of sunlight, falling thro' the veils
Of quivering poplars, lights upon her hair,
Shot golden, and across her candid brow.
Thus in the pleasant gloom she holds the eye,
Being life amid piled up remembrances
Of the tranquil dead.
        One hand, dropped lightly down,
Rests on the words of a forgotten name :
Therefore the past makes glad to stay her up.
Closed in, walled off : here's an oblivious place,
Deep, planted in with trees, unvisited :
A still backwater in the tide of life.

Life flows all round; sounds from surrounding
    streets,
Laughter of unseen children, roll of wheels,
Cries of all vendors.—So she sits and waits.
And she rejoices us who pass her by,
And she rejoices those who here lie still,
And she makes glad the little wandering airs,
And doth make glad the shaken beams of light
That fall upon her forehead : all the world
Moves round her, sitting on forgotten tombs
And lighting in to-morrow. She is Life :
That makes us keep on moving, taking roads,
Hauling great burdens up the unending hills,
Pondering senseless problems, setting sail
For undiscovered anchorages. Here
She waits, she waits, sequestered among tombs,
The sunlight on her hair. She waits, she waits :
The secret music, the resolving note
That sets in tune all this discordant world
And solves the riddles of the Universe.

Ford Madox Hueffer

THE SONG OF THE WOMEN

A Wealden Trio

1st Voice

WHEN ye've got a child 'ats whist for want of food,
And a grate as grey's y'r 'air for want of wood,
And y'r man and you ain't nowise not much good ;

Together

Oh—
It's hard work a-Christmassing,
Carolling,
Singin' songs about the " Babe what's born."

But, while the slow hours go,
I, who must fall before you, late shall wait and keep
    Watch and ward,
    Vigil and guard,
    Where you sleep.
Ah, sweet! do you the like where I lie dead.

            Ford Madox Hueffer

SONG OF POPLARS

SHEPHERD, to yon tall poplars tune your flute:
Let them pierce, keenly, subtly shrill,
The slow blue rumour of the hill;
Let the grass cry with an anguish of evening gold,
And the great sky be mute.

Then hearken how the poplar trees unfold
Their buds, yet close and gummed and blind,
In airy leafage of the mind,
Rustling in silvery whispers the twin-hued scales
That fade not nor grow old.

"Poplars and fountains and you cypress spires
Springing in dark and rusty flame,
Seek you aught that hath a name?
Or say, say: Are you all an upward agony
Of undefined desires?

"Say, are you happy in the golden march
Of sunlight all across the day?
Or do you watch the uncertain way
That leads the withering moon on cloudy stairs
Over the heaven's wide arch?

" Is it towards sorrow or towards joy you lift
The sharpness of your trembling spears ?
Or do you seek, through the grey tears
That blur the sky, in the heart of the triumphing
    blue,
A deeper, calmer rift ? "

So ; I have tuned my music to the trees,
And there were voices dim below
Their shrillness, voices swelling slow
In the blue murmur of hills, and a golden cry
And then vast silences.

Aldous Huxley

TAM I' THE KIRK

O JEAN, my Jean, when the bell ca's the congre-
    gation
    Owre valley an' hill wi' the ding frae its iron mou',
When a' body's thochts is set on his ain salvation,
    Mine's set on you.

There's a reid rose lies on the Buik o' the Word
    'afore ye
    That was growin' braw on its bush at the keek
    o' day,
But the lad that pu'd yon flower i' the mornin's
    glory,
    He canna pray.

He canna pray ; but there's nane i' the Kirk will
    heed him
    Whaur he sits sae still his lane at the side o' the
    wa',

King, tried in fires of woe!
　Men hunger for thy grace:
And through the night I go,
　Loving thy mournful face.

Yet, when the city sleeps;
　When all the cries are still:
The stars and heavenly deeps
　Work out a perfect will.

Lionel Johnson

IN MEMORY

Ah! fair face gone from sight,
　With all its light
Of eyes, that pierced the deep
　Of human night!
Ah! fair face calm in sleep.

Ah! fair lips hushed in death!
　Now their glad breath
Breathes not upon our air
　Music, that saith
Love only, and things fair.

Ah! lost brother! Ah! sweet
　Still hands and feet!
May those feet haste to reach,
　Those hands to greet
Us where love needs no speech.

Lionel Johnson

THE FLOWERS

Buy my English posies!
  Kent and Surrey may—
Violets of the Undercliff
  Wet with Channel spray;
Cowslips from a Devon combe—
  Midland furze afire—
Buy my English posies
  And I'll sell your heart's desire!

Buy my English posies!
  You that scorn the May,
Won't you greet a friend from home
  Half the world away?
Green against the draggled drift,
  Faint and frail and first—
Buy my Northern blood-root
    And I'll know where you were nursed!
Robin down the logging-road whistles, " Come to
    me ! "
Spring has found the maple-grove, the sap is running
    free ;
All the winds of Canada call the ploughing-rain.
Take the flower and turn the hour, and kiss your love
    again !

Buy my English posies!
  Here's to match your need—
Buy a tuft of royal heath,
  Buy a bunch of weed
White as sand of Muysenberg
  Spun before the gale—
Buy my heath and lilies
    And I'll tell you whence you hail!

9

Under hot Constantia broad the vineyards lie—
Throned and thorned the aching berg props the
    speckless sky—
Slow below the Wynberg firs trails the tilted wain—
Take the flower and turn the hour, and kiss your
    love again!

    Buy my English posies!
      You that will not turn—
    Buy my hot-wood clematis,
      Buy a frond o' fern
    Gather'd where the Erskine leaps
      Down the road to Lorne—
    Buy my Christmas creeper
      And I'll say where you were born!

West away from Melbourne dust holidays begin—
They that mock at Paradise woo at Cora Lynn—
Through the great South Otway gums sings the
    great South Main—
Take the flower and turn the hour, and kiss your
    love again!

    Buy my English posies!
      Here's your choice unsold!
    Buy a blood-red myrtle-bloom,
      Buy the kowhai's gold
    Flung for gift on Taupo's face,
      Sign that spring is come—
    Buy my clinging myrtle
      And I'll give you back your home!

Broom behind the windy town; pollen o' the pine—
Bell-bird in the leafy deep where the *ratas* twine—
Fern above the saddle-bow, flax upon the plain—
Take the flower and turn the hour, and kiss your
    love again!

Buy my English posies!
   Ye that have your own
Buy them for a brother's sake
   Overseas, alone.
Weed ye trample underfoot
   Floods his heart abrim—
Bird ye never heeded,
   O, she calls his dead to him.

Far and far our homes are set round the Seven Seas;
Woe for us if we forget, we that hold by these!
Unto each his mother-beach, bloom and bird and
   land—
Masters of the Seven Seas, oh, love and understand!

Rudyard Kipling

IF——

IF you can keep your head when all about you
   Are losing theirs and blaming it on you,
If you can trust yourself when all men doubt you,
   But make allowance for their doubting too;
If you can wait and not be tired by waiting,
   Or being lied about, don't deal in lies,
Or being hated, don't give way to hating,
   And yet don't look too good, nor talk too wise:

If you can dream—and not make dreams your
      master;
   If you can think—and not make thoughts your
      aim;
If you can meet with Triumph and Disaster
   And treat those two impostors just the same;
If you can bear to hear the truth you've spoken
   Twisted by knaves to make a trap for fools,
Or watch the things you gave your life to, broken,
   And stoop and build 'em up with worn-out tools:

If you can make one heap of all your winnings
    And risk it on one turn of pitch-and-toss,
And lose, and start again at your beginnings
    And never breathe a word about your loss;
If you can force your heart and nerve and sinew
    To serve your turn long after they are gone,
And so hold on when there is nothing in you
    Except the Will which says to them : " Hold on ! "

If you can talk with crowds and keep your virtue,
    Or walk with Kings—nor lose the common
        touch,
If neither foes nor loving friends can hurt you,
    If all men count with you, but none too much ;
If you can fill the unforgiving minute
    With sixty seconds' worth of distance run,
Yours is the Earth and everything that's in it,
    And—which is more—you'll be a Man, my son !
                 Rudyard Kipling

FEAR

ERE Mor the Peacock flutters, ere the Monkey
    People cry,
    Ere Chil the Kite swoops down a furlong sheer,
Through the Jungle very softly flits a Shadow and
    a sigh—
    He is Fear, O Little Hunter, he is Fear !
Very softly down the glade runs a waiting, watching
    shade,
    And the whisper spreads and widens far and near.
And the sweat is on thy brow, for he passes even
    now—
    He is Fear, O Little Hunter, he is Fear !

Ere the Moon has climbed the mountain, ere the
    rocks are ribbed with light,
  When the downward-dipping tails are dank and
    drear ;
Comes a breathing hard behind thee—*snuffle-*
    snuffle through the night—
  It is Fear, O Little Hunter, it is Fear !
On thy knees and draw the bow ; bid the shrilling
    arrow go ;
  In the empty, mocking thicket plunge the spear !
But thy hands are loosed and weak, and the blood
    has left thy cheek—
  It is Fear, O Little Hunter, it is Fear !

When the heat-cloud sucks the tempest, when the
    slivered pine trees fall,
  When the blinding, blaring rain-squalls lash and
    veer,
Through the war-gongs of the thunder rings a voice
    more loud than all—
  It is Fear, O Little Hunter, it is Fear !
Now the spates are banked and deep ; now the
    footless boulders leap—
  Now the lightning shows each littlest leaf-rib
    clear—
But thy throat is shut and dried, and thy heart
    against thy side
  Hammers : Fear, O Little Hunter—this is Fear !
                 Rudyard Kipling

RECESSIONAL

God of our fathers, known of old,
　Lord of our far-flung battle-line,
Beneath whose awful Hand we hold
　Dominion over palm and pine—
Lord God of Hosts, be with us yet,
Lest we forget—lest we forget!

The tumult and the shouting dies;
　The captains and the kings depart:
Still stands Thine ancient sacrifice,
　An humble and a contrite heart.
Lord God of Hosts, be with us yet,
Lest we forget—lest we forget!

Far-called, our navies melt away;
　On dune and headland sinks the fire:
Lo, all our pomp of yesterday
　Is one with Nineveh and Tyre!
Judge of the Nations, spare us yet,
Lest we forget—lest we forget!

If, drunk with sight of power, we loose
　Wild tongues that have not Thee in awe,
Such boasting as the Gentiles use,
　Or lesser breeds without the Law—
Lord God of Hosts, be with us yet,
Lest we forget—lest we forget!

For heathen heart that puts her trust
　In reeking tube and iron shard,
All valiant dust that builds on dust
　And, guarding, calls not Thee to guard,
For frantic boast and foolish word—
Thy Mercy on Thy People, Lord!　Amen.
　　　　　　　　　　　Rudyard Kipling

THE ODYSSEY

As one that for a weary space has lain
    Lull'd by the song of Circe and her wine
    In gardens near the pale of Proserpine,
Where that Æean isle forgets the main,
And only the low lutes of love complain,
    And only shadows of wan lovers pine,
    As such an one were glad to know the brine
Salt on his lips, and the large air again,
So gladly, from the songs of modern speech
    Men turn, and see the stars, and feel the free
        Shrill wind beyond the close of heavy flowers
        And through the music of the languid hours,
They hear like Ocean on a western beach
    The surge and thunder of the Odyssey.

Andrew Lang

GIORNO DEI MORTI

ALONG the avenue of cypresses,
All in their scarlet cloaks, and surplices
Of linen, go the chanting choristers,
The priests in gold and black, the villagers . . .

And all along the path to the cemetery
The round dark heads of men crowd silently,
And black-scarved faces of women-folk, wistfully
Watch at the banner of death, and the mystery.

And at the foot of a grave a father stands
With sunken head, and forgotten, folded hands;
And at the foot of a grave a mother kneels
With pale shut face, and neither hears nor feels

The coming of the chanting choristers
Between the avenue of cypresses,
The silence of the many villagers,
The candle-flames beside the surplices.

D. H. Lawrence

THE LOST ONES

SOMEWHERE is music from the linnets' bills,
And thro' the sunny flowers the bee-wings drone,
And white bells of convolvulus on hills
Of quiet May make silent ringing, blown
Hither and thither by the wind of showers,
And somewhere all the wandering birds have flown ;
And the brown breath of Autumn chills the flowers.

But where are all the loves of long ago ?
Oh, little twilight ship blown up the tide,
Where are the faces laughing in the glow
Of morning years, the lost ones scattered wide ?
Give me your hand, O brother, let us go
Crying about the dark for those who died.

Francis Ledwidge

SUPPLICATION

O YOU that on a Summer's day,
Upon the shores of Blacksod Bay,
Among the sunshine and the showers,
I called the shepherds of the flowers ;
The sturdy, sunburnt legs of you,
The round straw hats, the smocks of blue,
The brown locks and the golden locks,
That went a-following their flocks !

Into your hands you gathered then
Such colours as wise-fingered men
Painted on cups in Queen Anne's day,
When ladies called their tea Bohea:
Mauve orchises in printed dresses,
Yellow hawkweed, purple vetches,
Woodruff white, geranium rose,
Milkwort bluest flower that grows:
But these, and twice as many more,
Lie far beneath Time's crystal floor,
And you, instead of mountain sheep,
The tamer Sussex kind must keep:
Run to your flocks that here await
Your care within a garden gate:
Here the dark violet sweetness spreads,
And snowdrops hang their snow-white heads,
With wallflowers, squills and primroses,
Candytuft and crocuses,
And many a jonquil's leafy crown
Thrusting greenness through earth's brown:
Run to your flocks, and say that one
Who as they love it loves the sun,
Humbly desires that they will make
Their Spring a late one for her sake.
Say that in weakness and long pain
More than a season she has lain
Holding in hope but one small thing:
She should be well to see the Spring.
Oh, say to them to stay their growth,
This would be charity not sloth:
Beseech them stay that she may share
Their beauty with the gentle air.
Why should they hasten? Winter still
Puts a coldness on the hill—

I wonder if my stripey shawl
Seems pleasant in your eyes at all,
I can assure you that your wings
Are most delightful things.

Sweet birds, I pray, be not severe,
Do not deplore our presence here,
We cannot all be goldfinches
In such a world as this.

The shaded lawn, the bordered flowers,
We'll call them yours instead of ours,
The pinks and the acacia tree
Shall own your sovereignty.

And, if you let us, we will prove
Our lowly and obsequious love,
And when your little grey-pates hatch
We'll help you to keep watch.

No prowling stranger cats shall come
About your high celestial home,
With dangerous sounds we'll chase them hence
And ask no recompense.

And he, the Ethiope of our house,
Slayer of beetle and of mouse,
Huge, lazy, fond, whom we love well—
Peter shall wear a bell.

Believe me, birds, you need not fear,
No cages or limed twigs are here,
We only ask to live with you
In this green garden, too.

And when in other shining summers
Our place is taken by new-comers,
We'll leave them with the house and hill
The goldfinches' good will.

Your dainty flights, your painted coats,
The silver mist that is your notes,
And all your sweet caressing ways
Shall decorate their days.

And never will the thought of spring
Visit our minds, but a gold wing
Will flash among the green and blue,
And we'll remember you.

Sylvia Lynd

TO MY COMRADES

You, who once dreamed on earth to make your
      mark,
And kindle beacons where its ways were dark;
  To whom, for the world that had no need of
        you,
    It once had seemed a little thing to die;
Who gave the world your best, and in return
No honour won and no reward could earn!
  Sad Comrade! we were shipmates in one crew,—
    Somewhere we sailed together, you and I.

O you of little faith, the promised heir
Of life eternal, mourning days that were;
  You, who to lift up one belovèd head
    Out of the dust and feel one presence nigh,—

By the first men swinging in trees by strong tails.
    Not till the last man fails,
    And the sun's fire pales,
Shall the embers of these flaming dreams be cold.
Whatever the year brings, he brings nothing new.

    Turn, turn the page !
It turns, and we, and the squirrel in his cage,
And the sun, and the moon, and the moon's salt
    tide ;
    And the earth turns too.
As flies on the rim of a wheel we ride
    From age round to age ;
And the dreams and the toys which make our pride
    Are an old heritage,
Worn properties from some primeval stage
    All curtained now from view. . . .
Whatever the year brings, he brings nothing new.

    Go through the door.
You shall find nothing that has not been before,
Nothing so bitter it will not be once more.
All this our sad estate was known of yore,
    In old worlds red with pain,
Borne by hearts sullen and sick as ours, through
Desperate, forgotten, other winters, when
    Tears fell, and hopes, and men,
And crowns, and cities, and blood, on a trampled
    plain,
And nations, and honour, and God, and always
    rain. . . .
And honour and hope and God rose up again,
    And like trees nations grew. . . .
Whatever the year brings, he brings nothing new.

Should some year suddenly bring something new,
We should grope as lost children, without a clue.
We should drift all amazed through such a queer
    And unimagined year.
Riding uncharted seas, a derelict crew,
Whistling in vain for the old winds that blew
From the old skies, we should seek far and near
    Some mark by which to steer,
And some known port, that we might sail thereto.
    Black nightmare and blind fear
    Shall seize and hold him who
In some year suddenly finds something new.
                  Rose Macaulay

A CONSECRATION

NOT of the princes and prelates with periwigged
    charioteers
Riding triumphantly laurelled to lap the fat of the
    years,—
Rather the scorned—the rejected—the men hemmed
    in with the spears;

The men of the tattered battalion which fights
    till it dies,
Dazed with the dust of the battle, the din and the
    cries,
The men with the broken heads and the blood
    running into their eyes.

Not the be-medalled Commander, beloved of the
    throne,
Riding cock-horse to parade when the bugles are
    blown,
But the lads who carried the koppie and cannot
    be known.
    10

Not the ruler for me, but the ranker, the tramp of
    the road,
The slave with the sack on his shoulders pricked
    on with the goad,
The man with too weighty a burden, too weary
    a load.

The sailor, the stoker of steamers, the man with
    the clout,
The chantyman bent at the halliards putting a
    tune to the shout,
The drowsy man at the wheel and the tired look-
    out.

Others may sing of the wine and the wealth and the
    mirth,
The portly presence of potentates goodly in
    girth ;—
Mine be the dirt and the dross, the dust and scum
    of the earth !

Theirs be the music, the colour, the glory, the
    gold ;
Mine be a handful of ashes, a mouthful of mould.
Of the maimed, of the halt and the blind in the
    rain and the cold—

Of these shall my songs be fashioned, my tale be
    told. Amen.

John Masefield

CARGOES

QUINQUIREME of Nineveh from distant Ophir
Rowing home to haven in sunny Palestine,
    With a cargo of ivory,
    And apes and peacocks,
Sandalwood, cedarwood, and sweet white wine.

Stately Spanish galleon coming from the Isthmus,
Dipping through the Tropics by the palm-green
    shores,
    With a cargo of diamonds,
    Emeralds, amethysts,
Topazes, and cinnamon, and gold moidores.

Dirty British coaster with a salt-caked smoke stack
Butting through the Channel in the mad March
    days,
    With a cargo of Tyne coal,
    Road rail, pig lead,
Firewood, ironware, and cheap tin trays.

John Masefield

THE WILD DUCK

TWILIGHT. Red in the West.
Dimness. A glow on the wood.
The teams plod home to rest.
The wild duck come to glean.
O souls not understood,
What a wild cry in the pool;
What things have the farm ducks seen
That they cry so—huddle and cry?

Only the soul that goes,
Eager. Eager. Flying.
Over the globe of the moon,
Over the wood that glows.
Wings linked. Necks a-strain.
A rush and a wild crying.

.   .   .   .   .

A cry of the long pain
In the reeds of a steel lagoon,
In a land that no man knows.

John Masefield

THE SEEKERS

FRIENDS and loves we have none, nor wealth nor
blessed abode,
But the hope of the City of God at the other end
of the road.

Not for us are content, and quiet, and peace of mind,
For we go seeking a city that we shall never find.

There is no solace on earth for us—for such as we—
Who search for a hidden city that we shall never
see.

Only the road and the dawn, the sun, the wind,
and the rain,
And the watch-fire under the stars, and sleep, and
the road again.

We seek the city of God, and the haunt where
beauty dwells,
And we find the noisy mart and the sound of burial
bells.

Never the golden city, where radiant people meet,
But the dolorous town where mourners are going
about the street.

We travel the dusty road till the light of the day
is dim,
And sunset shows us spires away on the world's rim.

We travel from dawn to dusk, till the day is past
and by,
Seeking the Holy City beyond the rim of the sky.

Friends and loves we have none, nor wealth nor
blest abode,
But the hope of the City of God at the other end
of the road.

John Masefield

BEAUTY

I HAVE seen dawn and sunset on moors and windy
   hills
Coming in solemn beauty like slow old tunes of
   Spain :
I have seen the lady April bringing the daffodils,
Bringing the springing grass and the soft warm
   April rain.

I have heard the song of the blossoms and the old
   chant of the sea,
And seen strange lands from under the arched white
   sails of ships ;
But the loveliest things of beauty God ever has
   showed to me
Are her voice, and her hair, and eyes, and the dear
   red curve of her lips.

John Masefield

THE SPIRIT OF SHAKESPEARE

THY greatest knew thee, Mother Earth ; unsoured
   He knew thy sons. He probed from hell to hell
Of human passions, but of love deflowered
   His wisdom was not, for he knew thee well.
Thence came the honeyed corner at his lips,
   The conquering smile wherein his spirit sails
Calm as the God who the white sea-wave whips,
   Yet full of speech and intershifting tales,
Close mirrors of us : thence had he the laugh
   We feel is thine : broad as ten thousand beeves
At pasture ! thence thy songs, that winnow chaff
   From grain, bid sick Philosophy's last leaves
Whirl, if they have no response—they enforced
To fatten Earth when from her soul divorced.

How smiles he at a generation ranked
    In gloomy noddings over life! They pass.
Not he to feed upon a breast unthanked,
    Or eye a beauteous face in a cracked glass.
But he can spy that little twist of brain
    Which moved some weighty leader of the blind
Unwitting 'twas the goad of personal pain,
    To view in curst eclipse our Mother's mind,
And show us of some rigid harridan
    The wretched bondmen till the end of time.
O lived the Master now to paint us Man,
    That little twist of brain would ring a chime
Of whence it came and what it caused, to start
Thunders of laughter, clearing air and heart.

George Meredith

DIRGE IN WOODS

A WIND sways the pines,
        And below
Not a breath of wild air;
Still as the mosses that glow
On the flooring and over the lines
Of the roots here and there.
The pine-tree drops its dead;
They are quiet, as under the sea.
Overhead, overhead
Rushes life in a race,
As the clouds the clouds chase;
        And we go,
And we drop like the fruits of the tree,
        Even we,
        Even so.

George Meredith

MARIAN

I

SHE can be as wise as we,
   And wiser when she wishes;
She can knit with cunning wit,
   And dress the homely dishes.
She can flourish staff or pen,
   And deal a wound that lingers;
She can talk the talk of men,
   And touch with thrilling fingers.

II

Match her ye across the sea,
   Natures fond and fiery;
Ye who zest the turtle's nest
   With the eagle's eyrie.
Soft and loving is her soul,
   Swift and lofty soaring;
Mixing with its dove-like dole
   Passionate adoring.

III

Such a she who'll match with me?
   In flying or pursuing,
Subtle wiles are in her smiles
   To set the world a-wooing.
She is steadfast as a star,
   And yet the maddest maiden:
She can wage a gallant war,
   And give the peace of Eden.
               George Meredith

THE FARMER'S BRIDE

THREE Summers since I chose a maid,
Too young maybe—but more's to do
At harvest-time than bide and woo.
    When us was wed she turned afraid
Of love and me and all things human ;
Like the shut of a winter's day.
Her smile went out, and 'twasn't a woman—
    More like a little frightened fay.
        One night, in the Fall, she runned away.

" Out 'mong the sheep, her be," they said,
'Should properly have been abed ;
But sure enough she wasn't there
Lying awake with her wide brown stare.
So over seven-acre field and up-along across the down
    We chased her, flying like a hare
Before our lanterns. To Church-Town
    All in a shiver and a scare
We caught her, fetched her home at last
And turned the key upon her, fast.

She does the work about the house
As well as most, but like a mouse :
    Happy enough to chat and play
    With birds and rabbits and such as they,
    So long as men-folk keep away.
" Not near, not near ! " her eyes beseech
When one of us comes within reach.
    The women say that beasts in stall
    Look round like children at her call.
    I've hardly heard her speak at all.

Shy as a leveret, swift as he,
Straight and slight as a young larch tree,
Sweet as the first wild violets, she,
To her wild self. But what to me?

The short days shorten and the oaks are brown,
  The blue smoke rises to the low grey sky,
One leaf in the still air falls slowly down,
  A magpie's spotted feathers lie
On the black earth spread white with rime,
The berries redden up to Christmas-time.
  What's Christmas time without there be
  Some other in the house than we!

  She sleeps up in the attic there
  Alone, poor maid. 'Tis but a stair
Betwixt us. Oh! my God! the down,
The soft young down of her, the brown,
The brown of her—her eyes, her hair, her hair!

Charlotte Mew

THE CHANGELING

TOLL no bell for me, dear Father, dear Mother,
    Waste no sighs;
There are my sisters, there is my little brother
  Who plays in the place called Paradise,
Your children all, your children for ever;
    But I, so wild,
Your disgrace, with the queer brown face, was
    never,
  Never, I know, but half your child!

In the garden at play, all day, last summer,
    Far and away I heard
The sweet " tweet-tweet " of a strange new-comer,
  The dearest, clearest call of a bird.

THE SHEPHERDESS

She walks—the lady of my delight—
   A shepherdess of sheep.
Her flocks are thoughts. She keeps them white;
   She guards them from the steep;
She feeds them on the fragrant height,
   And folds them in for sleep.

She roams maternal hills and bright,
   Dark valleys safe and deep;
Into that tender breast at night
   The chastest stars may peep.
She walks—the lady of my delight—
   A shepherdess of sheep.

She holds her little thoughts in sight,
   Though gay they run and leap.
She is so circumspect and right;
   She has her soul to keep.
She walks—the lady of my delight—
   A shepherdess of sheep.

Alice Meynell

CHRIST IN THE UNIVERSE

With this ambiguous earth
His dealings have been told us. These abide:
The signal to a maid, the human birth,
The lesson, and the young Man crucified.

   But not a star of all
The innumerable host of stars has heard
How He administered this terrestrial ball.
Our race have kept their Lord's entrusted Word.

Of His earth-visiting feet
None knows the secret, cherished, perilous,
The terrible, shamefast, frightened, whispered,
    sweet,
Heart-shattering secret of His way with us.

No planet knows that this
Our wayside planet, carrying land and wave,
Love and life multiplied, and pain and bliss,
Bears, as chief treasure, one forsaken grave.

Nor, in our little day,
May His devices with the heavens be guessed,
His pilgrimage to thread the Milky Way,
Or His bestowals there, be manifest.

But, in the eternities,
Doubtless we shall compare together, hear
A million alien gospels, in what guise
He trod the Pleiades, the Lyre, the Bear.

Oh be prepared, my soul!
To read the inconceivable, to scan
The infinite forms of God those stars unroll
When, in our turn, we show to them a Man.

Alice Meynell

"I AM THE WAY"

Thou art the Way.
Hadst Thou been nothing but the goal
    I cannot say
If Thou hadst ever met my soul.

I cannot see—
I, child of process—if there lies
    An end for me,
Full of repose, full of replies.

("Will you not play?
Jesus, run to him, run to him, swift for our joy.
Is he not holy, like you?
Are you afraid of his arrows, O beautiful dreaming
        boy?")

And now they stand
Watching one another with timid gaze;
Youth has met youth in the wood,
But holiness will not change its melancholy ways.

Cupid at last
Draws his bow and softly lets fly a dart.
Smile for a moment, sad world!—
It has grazed the white skin and drawn blood from
        the sorrowful heart.

Now, for delight,
Cupid tosses his locks and goes wantonly near;
But the child that was born to the cross
Has let fall on his cheek, for the sadness of life, a
        compassionate tear.

Marvellous dream!
Cupid has offered his arrows for Jesus to try;
He has offered his bow for the game.
But Jesus went weeping away, and left him there
        wondering why.

                                    Harold Monro

SOLITUDE

WHEN you have tidied all things for the night,
    And while your thoughts are fading to their
        sleep,

You'll pause a moment in the late firelight,
  Too sorrowful to weep.

The large and gentle furniture has stood
  In sympathetic silence all the day
With that old kindness of domestic wood;
  Nevertheless the haunted room will say:
  " Some one must be away."

The little dog rolls over half awake,
  Stretches his paws, yawns, looking up at you,
Wags his tail very slightly for your sake,
  That you may feel he is unhappy too.

A distant engine whistles, or the floor
Creaks, or the wandering night-wind bangs a door.

Silence is scattered like a broken glass.
  The minutes prick their ears and run about,
Then one by one subside again and pass
  Sedately in, monotonously out.

You bend your head and wipe away a tear.
Solitude walks one heavy step more near.

                              Harold Monro

MILK FOR THE CAT

WHEN the tea is brought at five o'clock,
  And all the neat curtains are drawn with care,
The little black cat with bright green eyes
  Is suddenly purring there.

At first she pretends, having nothing to do,
  She has come in merely to blink by the grate,
But, though tea may be late or the milk may be sour,
  She is never late.

  II

And presently her agate eyes
   Take a soft large milky haze,
And her independent casual glance
   Becomes a stiff hard gaze.

Then she stamps her claws or lifts her ears
   Or twists her tail or begins to stir,
Till suddenly all her lithe body becomes
   One breathing trembling purr.

The children eat and wriggle and laugh;
   The two old ladies stroke their silk:
But the cat is grown small and thin with desire,
   Transformed to a creeping lust for milk.

The white saucer like some full moon descends
   At last from the clouds of the table above;
She sighs and dreams and thrills and glows,
   Transfigured with love.

She nestles over the shining rim,
   Buries her chin in the creamy sea;
Her tail hangs loose; each drowsy paw
   Is doubled under each bending knee.

A long, dim ecstasy holds her life;
   Her world is an infinite shapeless white,
Till her tongue has curled the last holy drop,
   Then she sinks back into the night,

Draws and dips her body to heap
   Her sleepy nerves in the great arm-chair,
Lies defeated and buried deep
   Three or four hours unconscious there.

Harold Monro

A DUET

" FLOWERS nodding gaily, scent in air,
Flowers posied, flowers for the hair,
Sleepy flowers, flowers bold to stare—"
    " O pick me some ! "

" Shells with lip, or tooth, or bleeding gum,
Tell-tale shells, and shells that whisper *Come*,
Shells that stammer, blush, and yet are dumb—"
    " O let me hear ! "

" Eyes so black they draw one trembling near,
Brown eyes, caverns flooded with a tear,
Cloudless eyes, blue eyes so windy clear—"
    " O look at me ! "

" Kisses sadly blown across the sea,
Darkling kisses, kisses fair and free,
Bob-a-cherry kisses 'neath a tree—"
    " O give me one ! "

Thus sang a king and queen in Babylon.
          T. Sturge Moore

TO IDLENESS

ENOUGH, thou witch, too fond of me,
  Begone, I know and hate thee !
Nothing canst thou of pleasure see
  In one that so doth rate thee :

For empty are both mind and heart
  While thou with me dost linger;
More profit would to thee impart
  A babe that sucks its finger.

I know thou hast a better way
  To spend these hours thou squanderest;
Some lad toils in the trough to-day
  Who groans because thou wanderest;

A bleating sheep he dowses now
  Or wrestles with ram's terror;
Ah, 'mid the washing's hubbub, how
  His sighs reproach thine error!

He knows and loves thee, Idleness;
  For when his sheep are browsing,
His open eyes enchant and bless
  A mind divinely drowsing;

No slave to sleep, he wills and sees
  From hill-lawns the brown tillage;
Green winding lanes and clumps of trees,
  Far town or nearer village,

The sea itself; the fishing fleet
  Where more as fond, thy lovers,
Heark'ning to sea-mews find thee sweet
  Like him who hears the plovers.

Begone; those haul their ropes at sea,
  These plunge sheep in yon river:
Free, free from toil thy friends, and me
  From Idleness deliver!

                              T. Sturge Moore

KINDNESS

Of the beauty of kindness I speak,
  Of a smile, of a charm
On the face it is pleasure to meet
  That gives no alarm!

Of the soul that absorbeth itself
  In discovering good,
Of that power which outlasts health,
  As the spell of a wood

Outlasts the sad fall of the leaves,
  And in winter is fine,
And from snow and from frost receives
  A garment divine.

Oh! well may the lark sing of this,
  As through rents of huge cloud,
He broacheth blue gulfs that are bliss,
  For they make his heart proud

With the power of wings deployed
  In delightfullest air.
Yea, thus among things enjoyed
  Is kindness rare.

For even the weak with surprise
  Spread wings, utter song,
They can launch—in this blue they can rise,
  In this kindness are strong,—

They can launch like a ship into calm,
  Which was penn'd up by storm,
Which sails for the islands of balm
  Luxuriant and warm.

                    T. Sturge Moore

THAT LAND

WOULD that I might live for ever
Where those who make me happy dwell!
Desire doeth excellently well,
Now, wooing me;
For, oh, she never
Nameth any other place!
There ease weds grace;
There thought is free,
Born like a smile upon the face,
Expressed as simply as a child
Kisseth its playmate, laughing gaily;
There, there, the courteous, joyous, mild
Train life to beauty daily!

There thought is free; for life is bound
Religiously, and sings while serving;
No inner echoes counsel swerving,
All strengthen life,
Till sought be found;
Old valours rise to share
Ordeals there;
Near, like a wife,
Stands effort's outcome bodied fair,
Not fettered with dead thoughts, not fainting
Because the night-mare world hath lain
Athwart her hopes, but love acquainting
With beauty ever again.

Ever again and again
Filling the eyes of our child
With the milk of paradise,—
Of which the soul is fain,

For which the heart is wild,
And tears are in the eyes :
Ah ! that milk of paradise
Is happiness,
Is power to bless ;
What balmy air to halcyon's wing
That power to those who make me glad is :
To bind my life, in bonds to sing,
The way such freedom may be had is ;—
The way to gain the power to bless,
The one way to win happiness.

T. Sturge Moore

TO EXILES

ARE you not weary in your distant places,
   Far, far from Scotland of the mist and storm,
In drowsy airs, the sun-smite on your faces,
   The days so long and warm ?
When all around you lie the strange fields sleeping,
   The dreary woods where no fond memories roam,
Do not your sad hearts over seas come leaping
   To the highlands and the lowlands of your Home ?

Wild cries the Winter, loud through all our valleys ;
   The midnights roar, the grey noons echo back ;
Round steep storm-bitten coasts the eager galleys
   Beat for kind harbours from horizons black ;
We tread the miry roads, the rain-drenched hea-
      ther,
   We are the men, we battle, we endure !
God's pity for you people in your weather
   Of swooning winds, calm seas, and skies demure !

Wild cries the Winter, and we walk song-haunted
 Over the moors and by the thundering falls,
Or where the dirge of a brave past is chaunted
 In dolorous dusks by immemorial walls.
Though rains may thrash on us, the great mists
 blind us,
 And lightning rend the pine-tree on the hill,
Yet are we strong, yet shall the morning find us
 Children of tempest all unshaken still.

We wander where the little grey towns cluster
 Deep in the hills, or selvedging the sea,
By farm-lands lone, by woods where wildfowl
 muster
 To shelter from the day's inclemency ;
And night will come, and then far through the
 darkling,
 A light will shine out in the sounding glen,
And it will mind us of some fond eye's sparkling,
 And we'll be happy then.

Let torrents pour then, let the great winds rally,
 Snow-silence fall or lightning blast the pine ;
That light of Home shines warmly in the valley,
 And, exiled son of Scotland, it is thine.
Far have you wandered over seas of longing,
 And now you drowse, and now you well may weep,
When all the recollections come a-thronging
 Of this rude country where your fathers sleep.

They sleep, but still the hearth is warmly glowing,
 While the wild Winter blusters round their land ;
That light of Home, the wind so bitter blowing—
 Do they not haunt your dreams on alien Strand ?

Love, strength, and tempest—oh, come back and
    share them !
  Here's the old cottage, here the open door ;
Fond are our hearts although we do not bare them,—
    They're yours, and you are ours for evermore.
                    Neil Munro

DRAKE'S DRUM

DRAKE he's in his hammock an' a thousand mile
    away,
  (Capten, art tha sleepin' there below ?),
Slung atween the round shot in Nombre Dios Bay
  An' dreamin' arl the time o' Plymouth Hoe.
Yarnder lumes the Island, yarnder lie the ships,
  Wi' sailor-lads a-dancin' heel-an'-toe,
An' the shore-lights flashin', and the night-tide
    dashin',
  He sees et arl so plainly as he saw et long ago.

Drake he was a Devon man, an' rüled the Devon
    seas,
  (Capten, art tha sleepin' there below ?),
Rovin' tho' his death fell, he went wi' heart at ease,
  An' dreamin' arl the time o' Plymouth Hoe.
" Take my drum to England, hang et by the shore,
  Strike et when your powder's runnin' low ;
If the Dons sight Devon, I'll quit the port o' Heaven,
  An' drum them up the channel as we drummed
    them long ago."

Drake he's in his hammock till the great Armadas
    come,
  (Capten, art tha sleepin' there below ?),
Slung atween the round shot, listenin' for the drum,
  An' dreamin' arl the time o' Plymouth Hoe.

He saw the April noon on his books aglow,
    The wistaria trailing in at the window wide ;
He heard his father's voice from the terrace below
    Calling him down to ride.

He saw the gray little church across the park,
    The mounds that hide the loved and honoured
        dead ;
The Norman arch, the chancel softly dark,
    The brasses black and red.

He saw the School Close, sunny and green,
    The runner beside him, the stand by the parapet
        wall,
The distant tape, and the crowd roaring between
    His own name over all.

He saw the dark wainscot and timbered roof,
    The long tables, and the faces merry and keen,
The College Eight and their trainer dining aloof,
    The Dons on the daïs serene.

He watch'd the liner's stem ploughing the foam,
    He felt her trembling speed and the thrash of
        her screw ;
He heard the passengers' voices talking of home,
    He saw the flag she flew.

And now it was dawn. He rose strong on his feet,
    And strode to his ruin'd camp below the wood ;
He drank the breath of the morning cool and sweet ;
    His murderers round him stood.

Light on the Laspur hills was broadening fast,
    The blood-red snow-peaks chilled to a dazzling
        white ;
He turn'd, and saw the golden circle at last,
    Cut by the Eastern height.

" O glorious Life, Who dwellest in earth and sun,
  I have lived, I praise and adore thee."
                              A sword swept.
Over the pass the voices one by one
  Faded, and the hill slept.

Henry Newbolt

BATTERY MOVING UP TO A NEW POSITION
FROM REST CAMP: DAWN

NOT a sign of life we rouse
In any square close-shuttered house
That flanks the road we amble down
Toward far trenches through the town.

The dark, snow-slushy, empty street. . . .
Tingle of frost in brow and feet. . . .
Horse-breath goes dimly up like smoke.
No sound but the smacking stroke

Of a sergeant who flings each arm
Out and across to keep him warm,
And the sudden splashing crack
Of ice-pools broken by our track.

More dark houses, yet no sign
Of life. . . . An axle's creak and whine. . . .
The splash of hooves, the strain of trace. . . .
Clatter: we cross the market place. . . .

Deep quiet again, and on we lurch
Under the shadow of a church:
Its tower ascends, fog-wreathed and grim;
Within its aisles a light burns dim. . . .

When, marvellous! from overhead,
Like abrupt speech of one deemed dead,
Speech-moved by some Superior Will,
A bell tolls thrice and then is still.

For, set in that tiny chamber, Jesus, the blessed and
    doomed,
Spoke to the lone apostles as light to men entombed ;
And spreading His hands in blessing, as one soon to
    be dead,
He put soft enchantment into spare wine and bread.

The hearts of the disciples were broken and full of
    tears,
Because their Lord, the spearless, was hedged about
    with spears ;
And in His face the sickness of departure had spread
    a gloom,
At leaving His young friends friendless.
                  They could not forget the tomb.
He smiled subduedly, telling, in tones soft as voice
    of the dove,
The endlessness of sorrow, the eternal solace of love ;
And lifting the earthly tokens, wine and sorrowful
    bread,
He bade them sup and remember One who lived and
    was dead.
And they could not restrain their weeping.
                  But one rose up to depart,
Having weakness and hate of weakness raging within
    his heart,
And bowed to the robed assembly whose eyes
    gleamed wet in the light.
Judas arose and departed : night went out to the
    night.

Then Jesus lifted His voice like a fountain in an
    ocean of tears,
And comforted His disciples and calmed and allayed
    their fears.

But Judas wound down the turret, creeping from
    floor to floor,
And would fly; but one leaning, weeping, barred
    him beside the door.
And he knew her by her ruddy garment and two
    yet-watching men:
Mary of Seven Evils, Mary Magdalen.
And he was frighted at her. She sighed: " I
    dreamed him dead.
We sell the body for silver. . . ."
            Then Judas cried out and fled
Forth into the night! . . . The moon had begun
    to set:
A drear, deft wind went sifting, setting the dust
    afret;
Into the heart of the city Judas ran on and prayed
To stern Jehovah lest his deed make him afraid.

But in the tiny lantern, hanging as if on air,
The disciples sat unspeaking. Amaze and peace
    were there.
For *His* voice, more lovely than song of all earthly
    birds,
In accents humble and happy spoke slow, consoling
    words.

Thus Jesus discoursed, and was silent, sitting up-
    right, and soon
Past the casement behind Him slanted the sinking
    moon;
And, rising for Olivet, all stared, between love and
    dread,
Seeing the torrid moon a ruddy halo behind his head.
                      Robert Nichols

THE ELFIN ARTIST

IN a glade of an elfin forest
   When Sussex was Eden-new,
I came on an elvish painter
   And watched as his picture grew.
A harebell nodded beside him.
   He dipt his brush in the dew.

And it might be the wild thyme round him
   That shone in that dark strange ring ;
But his brushes were bees' antennae,
   His knife was a wasp's blue sting ;
And his gorgeous exquisite palette
   Was a butterfly's fan-shaped wing.

And he mingled its powdery colours,
   And painted the lights that pass,
On a delicate cobweb canvas
   That gleamed like a magic glass,
And bloomed like a banner of elf-land,
   Between two stalks of grass ;

Till it shone like an angel's feather
   With sky-born opal and rose,
And gold from the foot of the rainbow,
   And colours that no man knows ;
And I laughed in the sweet May weather,
   Because of the themes he chose.

For he painted the things that matter,
   The tints that we all pass by,
Like the little blue wreaths of incense
   That the wild thyme breathes to the sky ;
Or the first white bud of the hawthorn,
   And the light in a blackbird's eye ;

And the shadows on soft white cloud-peaks
　　That carolling skylarks throw,—
Dark dots on the slumbering splendours
　　That under the wild wings flow,
Wee shadows like violets trembling
　　On the unseen breasts of snow;

With petals too lovely for colour
　　That shake to the rapturous wings,
And grow as the bird draws near them,
　　And die as he mounts and sings;—
Ah, only those exquisite brushes
　　Could paint these marvellous things.

Alfred Noyes

GRACE FOR LIGHT

WHEN we were little childer we had a quare wee
　　house,
　　Away up in the heather by the head o' Brabla'
　　　burn;
The hares we'd see them scootin', an' we'd hear the
　　crowin' grouse,
　　An' when we'd all be in at night ye'd not get
　　　room to turn.

The youngest two She'd put to bed, their faces to
　　the wall,
　　An' the lave of us could sit aroun', just anywhere
　　　we might;
Herself 'ud take the rush-dip an' light it for us all,
　　An' " <i>God be thankèd !</i> " she would say,—" <i>now,
　　we have a light.</i>"

Then we be to quet the laughin' an' pushin' on the
floor,
> An' think on One who called us to come and be
> forgiven ;
Himself 'ud put his pipe down, an' say the good
word more,
> " *May the Lamb o' God lead us all to the Light o'*
> *Heaven !* "

There's a wheen things that used to be an' now has
had their day,
> The nine glens of Antrim can show ye many a
> sight ;
But not the quare wee house where we lived up
Brabla' way,
> Nor a child in all the nine Glens that knows the
> grace for light.

Moira O'Neill

CORRYMEELA

OVER here in England I'm helpin' wi' the hay,
An' I wisht I was in Ireland the livelong day ;
Weary on the English hay, an' sorra take the wheat !
> *Och ! Corrymeela an' the blue sky over it.*

There's a deep dumb river flowin' by beyont the
heavy trees,
This livin' air is moithered wi' the bummin' o' the
bees ;
I wisht I'd hear the Claddagh burn go runnin'
through the heat
> *Past Corrymeela, wi' the blue sky over it.*

The people that's in England is richer nor the Jews,
There's not the smallest young gossoon but thravels
in his shoes!
I'd give the pipe between me teeth to see a barefut
child,
   Och! Corrymeela an' the low south wind.

Here's hands so full o' money an' hearts so full o'
care,
By the luck o' love! I'd still go light for all I did
go bare,
" God save ye, *colleen dhas*," I said : the girl she
thought me wild.
   Far Corrymeela, an' the low south wind.

D'ye mind me now, the song at night is mortial
hard to raise,
The girls are heavy goin' here, the boys are ill to
plase ;
When one'st I'm out this workin' hive, 'tis I'll be
back again—
   Ay, Corrymeela, in the same soft rain.

The puff o' smoke from one ould roof before an
English town!
For a shaugh wid Andy Feelan here I'd give a silver
crown,
For a curl o' hair like Mollie's ye'll ask the like in
vain,
   Sweet Corrymeela, an' the same soft rain.
                       Moira O'Neill

A PIPER

A PIPER in the streets to-day
Set up, and tuned, and started to play,
And away, away, away on the tide
Of his music we started; on every side
Doors and windows were opened wide,
And men left down their work and came,
And women with petticoats coloured like flame
And little bare feet that were blue with cold,
Went dancing back to the age of gold,
And all the world went gay, went gay,
For half an hour in the street to-day.

Seumas O'Sullivan

MINERS

THERE was a whispering in my hearth,
  A sigh of the coal,
Grown wistful of a former earth
  It might recall.

I listened for a tale of leaves
  And smothered ferns;
Frond-forests; and the low, sly lives
  Before the fawns

My fire might show steam-phantoms simmer
  From Time's old cauldron,
Before the birds made nests in summer,
  Or men had children.

But the coals were murmuring of their mine,
  And moans down there
Of boys that slept wry sleep, and men
  Writhing for air.

And I saw white bones in the cinder-shard.
    Bones without number ;
For many hearts with coal are charred
    And few remember.

I thought of some who worked dark pits
    Of war, and died
Digging the rock where Death reputes
    Peace lies indeed :

Comforted years will sit soft-chaired,
    In rooms of amber ;
The years will stretch their hands, well-cheered
    By our life's ember ;

The centuries will burn rich loads
    With which we groaned,
Whose warmth shall lull their dreaming lids
    While songs are crooned ;
But they will not dream of us poor lads
    Lost in the ground.

Wilfred Owen

GREATER LOVE

RED lips are not so red
    As the stained stones kissed by the English dead.
Kindness of wooed and wooer
Seems shame to their love pure.
O Love, your eyes lose lure
    When I behold eyes blinded in my stead !

Your slender attitude
    Trembles not exquisite like limbs knife-skewed,
Rolling and rolling there
Where God seems not to care ;
Till the fierce Love they bear
    Cramps them in death's extreme decrepitude.

Your voice sings not so soft,—
   Though even as wind murmuring through
     raftered loft,—
Your dear voice is not dear,
Gentle, and evening clear,
As theirs whom none now hear,
   Now earth has stopped their piteous mouths
     that coughed.

Heart, you were never hot,
   Nor large, nor full like hearts made great with shot;
And though your hand be pale,
Paler are all which trail
Your cross through flame and hail:
   Weep, you may weep, for you may touch them
     not.

Wilfred Owen

ANTHEM FOR DOOMED YOUTH

WHAT passing-bells for these who die as cattle?
   Only the monstrous anger of the guns.
   Only the stuttering rifles' rapid rattle
Can patter out their hasty orisons.
No mockeries for them from prayers or bells,
Nor any voice of mourning save the choirs,—
The shrill, demented choirs of wailing shells;
And bugles calling for them from sad shires.

What candles may be held to speed them all?
   Not in the hands of boys, but in their eyes
Shall shine the holy glimmers of good-byes.
   The pallor of girls' brows shall be their pall;
Their flowers the tenderness of patient minds,
And each slow dusk a drawing-down of blinds.

Wilfred Owen

STRANGE MEETING

It seemed that out of the battle I escaped
Down some profound dull tunnel, long since scooped
Through granites which Titanic wars had groined.
Yet also there encumbered sleepers groaned,
Too fast in thought or death to be bestirred.
Then, as I probed them, one sprang up, and stared
With piteous recognition in fixed eyes,
Lifting distressful hands as if to bless.
And by his smile, I knew that sullen hall,
By his dead smile I knew we stood in Hell.
With a thousand pains that vision's face was grained ;
Yet no blood reached there from the upper ground,
And no guns thumped, or down the flues made moan.
" Strange friend," I said, " here is no cause to
    mourn."
" None," said the other, " save the undone years,
The hopelessness. Whatever hope is yours,
Was my life also ; I went hunting wild
After the wildest beauty in the world,
Which lies not calm in eyes, or braided hair,
But mocks the steady running of the hour,
And if it grieves, grieves richlier than here.
For by my glee might many men have laughed,
And of my weeping something had been left,
Which must die now. I mean the truth untold,
The pity of war, the pity war distilled.
Now men will go content with what we spoiled.
Or, discontent, boil bloody, and be spilled.
They will be swift with swiftness of the tigress,
None will break ranks, though nations trek from
    progress.
Courage was mine, and I had mystery,
Wisdom was mine, and I had mastery ;

PLYMOUTH

Composed at dawn in the Bay of Naples

Oh! what know they of harbours
  Who toss not on the sea?
They tell of fairer havens,
  But none so fair there be

As Plymouth town outstretching
  Her quiet arms to me,
Her breast's broad welcome spreading
  From Mewstone to Penlee.

And with this home-thought, darling,
  Come crowding thoughts of thee;
Oh! what know they of harbours
  Who toss not on the sea?

Ernest Radford

A CONCERT PARTY

(EGYPTIAN BASE CAMP)

They are gathering round . . .
Out of the twilight; over the grey-blue sand,
Shoals of low-jargoning men drift inward to the
    sound,—
The jangle and throb of a piano . . . tum-ti-tum. . . .
Drawn by a lamp, they come
Out of the glimmering lines of their tents, over the
    shuffling sand.

O sing us the songs, the songs of our own land,
You warbling ladies in white.
Dimness conceals the hunger in our faces,
This wall of faces risen out of the night,
These eyes that keep their memories of the places
So long beyond their sight.

Jaded and gay, the ladies sing; and the chap in
    brown
Tilts his grey hat; jaunty and lean and pale,
He rattles the keys. . . . Some actor-bloke from
    town . . .
God send you home; and then *A long, long trail;*
I hear you calling me; and *Dixieland*. . . .
Sing slowly . . . now the chorus . . . one by one
We hear them, drink them; till the concert's done.
Silent, I watch the shadowy mass of soldiers stand.
Silent, they drift away over the glimmering sand.
   Kantara, *April,* 1918.   *Siegfried Sassoon*

EVERYONE SANG

EVERYONE suddenly burst out singing;
And I was filled with such delight
As prisoned birds must find in freedom
Winging wildly across the white
Orchards and dark-green fields; on; on; and out
    of sight.

Everyone's voice was suddenly lifted,
And beauty came like the setting sun.
My heart was shaken with tears and horror
Drifted away . . . O, but everyone
Was a bird; and the song was wordless; the
    singing will never be done.
                 Siegfried Sassoon

The Lord held his head fast, and you could see
That He kissed the unsheathed ghost that was gone
    free—
As a hot sun, on a March day, kisses the cold ground ;
And the spirit answered, for he knew well that his
    peace was found.

The spirit trembled, and sprang up at the Lord's
    word—
As on a wild, April day springs a small bird—
So, the ghost's feet lifting him up, he kissed the
    Lord's cheek,
And for the greatness of their love neither of them
    could speak.

But the Lord went then, to show him the way,
Over the young crocuses, under the green may
That was not quite in flower yet—to a far-distant
    land ;
And the ghost followed, like a naked cloud holding
    the sun's hand.

Fredegond Shove

THE COMFORTERS

WHEN I crept over the hill, broken with tears,
    When I crouched down on the grass, dumb in
    despair,
I heard the soft croon of the wind bend to my ears,
    I felt the light kiss of the wind touching my hair.

When I stood lone on the height my sorrow did
    speak,
    As I went down the hill, I cried and I cried,
The soft little hands of the rain stroking my cheek,
    The kind little feet of the rain ran by my side.

When I went to thy grave, broken with tears,
  When I crouched down in the grass, dumb in
    despair,
I heard the sweet croon of the wind soft in my ears,
  I felt the kind lips of the wind touching my hair.

When I stood lone by thy cross, sorrow did speak,
  When I went down the long hill, I cried and I
    cried.
The soft little hands of the rain stroked my pale
    cheek,
  The kind little feet of the rain ran by my side.

Dora Sigerson

THE SONG OF THE UNGIRT RUNNERS

We swing ungirded hips,
  And lightened are our eyes,
The rain is on our lips,
  We do not run for prize.
We know not whom we trust
  Nor whitherward we fare,
But we run because we must
  Through the great wide air.

The waters of the seas
  Are troubled as by storm.
The tempest strips the trees
  And does not leave them warm.
Does the tearing tempest pause?
  Do the tree-tops ask it why?
So we run without a cause
  'Neath the big bare sky.

The rain is on our lips,
    We do not run for prize.
But the storm the water whips
    And the wave howls to the skies.
The winds arise and strike it
    And scatter it like sand,
And we run because we like it
        Through the broad bright land.

Charles Hamilton Sorley

EXPECTANS EXPECTAVI

FROM morn to midnight, all day through,
I laugh and play as others do,
I sin and chatter, just the same
As others with a different name.

And all year long upon the stage
I dance and tumble and do rage
So vehemently, I scarcely see
The inner and eternal me.

I have a temple I do not
Visit, a heart I have forgot,
A self that I have never met,
A secret shrine—and yet, and yet

This sanctuary of my soul
Unwitting I keep white and whole
Unlatched and lit, if Thou should'st care
To enter or to tarry there.

With parted lips and outstretched hands
And listening ears Thy servant stands,
Call Thou early, call Thou late,
To Thy great service dedicate.

Charles Hamilton Sorley

THE SHIP

THERE was no song nor shout of joy
  Nor beam of moon or sun,
When she came back from the voyage
  Long ago begun ;
But twilight on the waters
  Was quiet and grey,
And she glided steady, steady and pensive,
  Over the open bay.

Her sails were brown and ragged,
  And her crew hollow-eyed,
But their silent lips spoke content
  And their shoulders pride ;
Though she had no captives on her deck,
  And in her hold
There were no heaps of corn or timber
  Or silks or gold.

J. C. Squire

WINTER NIGHTFALL

THE old yellow stucco
Of the time of the Regent
Is flaking and peeling :
The rows of square windows
In the straight yellow building
  Are empty and still ;
And the dusty dark evergreens
Guarding the wicket
Are draped with wet cobwebs,
And above this poor wilderness
Toneless and sombre
  Is the flat of the hill.

TO A BULL-DOG

(W.H.S., Capt. (Acting Major) R.F.A.; *killed*
April 12, 1917)

We shan't see Willy any more, Mamie,
   He won't be coming any more:
He came back once and again and again,
   But he won't get leave any more.

We looked from the window and there was his cab,
   And we ran downstairs like a streak,
And he said "Hullo, you bad dog," and you
     crouched to the floor,
   Paralysed to hear him speak,

And then let fly at his face and his chest
   Till I had to hold you down,
While he took off his cap and his gloves and his coat
   And his bag and his thonged Sam Browne.

We went upstairs to the studio,
   The three of us, just as of old,
And you lay down and I sat and talked to him
   As round the room he strolled.

Here in this room where, years ago
   Before the old life stopped,
He worked all day with his slippers and his pipe,
   He would pick up the threads he'd dropped,

Fondling all the drawings he had left behind,
   Glad to find them all still the same,
And opening the cupboards to look at his belongings
   . . . Every time he came.

But now I know what a dog doesn't know,
  Though you'll thrust your head on my knee,
And try to draw me from the absent-mindedness
  That you find so dull in me.

And all your life you will never know
  What I wouldn't tell you even if I could,
That the last time we waved him away
  Willy went for good.

But sometimes as you lie on the hearthrug
  Sleeping in the warmth of the stove,
Even through your muddled old canine brain
  Shapes from the past may rove.

You'll scarcely remember, even in a dream,
  How we brought home a silly little pup,
With a big square head and little crooked legs
  That could scarcely bear him up,

But your tail will tap at the memory
  Of a man whose friend you were,
Who was always kind though he called you a
    naughty dog
  When he found you on his chair;

Who'd make you face a reproving finger
  And solemnly lecture you
Till your head hung downwards and you looked
    very sheepish !
  And you'll dream of your triumphs too.

Of summer evening chases in the garden
  When you dodged us all about with a bone :
We were three boys, and you were the cleverest,
  But now we're two alone.

When summer comes again,
  And the long sunsets fade,
We shall have to go on playing the feeble game for
    two
  That since the war we've played.

And though you run expectant as you always do
  To the uniforms we meet,
You'll never find Willy among all the soldiers
  In even the longest street,

Nor in any crowd ; yet, strange and bitter thought,
  Even now were the old words said,
If I tried the old trick and said " Where's Willy ? "
  You would quiver and lift your head,

And your brown eyes would look to ask if I were
    serious,
  And wait for the word to spring.
Sleep undisturbed : I shan't say *that* again,
    You innocent old thing.

I must sit, not speaking, on the sofa,
  While you lie asleep on the floor ;
For he's suffered a thing that dogs couldn't dream of,
  And he won't be coming here any more.

J. C. Squire

IN THE POPPY FIELD

Mad Patsy said, he said to me,
That every morning he could see
An angel walking on the sky ;
Across the sunny skies of morn

He threw great handfuls far and nigh
Of poppy seed among the corn ;
—And then, he said, the angels run
To see the poppies in the sun—

—A poppy is a devil weed,—
I said to him—he disagreed :
He said the devil had no hand
In spreading flowers tall and fair
By corn and rye and meadow land,
By gurth and barrow everywhere :
The devil has not any flower,
But only money in his power.

And then he stretched out in the sun
And rolled upon his back for fun !
He kicked his legs and roared for joy
Because the sun was shining down !
He said he was a little boy
And wouldn't work for any clown !
He ran and laughed behind a bee ;
And danced for very ecstasy !

James Stephens

THE SNARE

I HEAR a sudden cry of pain !
    There is a rabbit in a snare :
Now I hear the cry again,
    But I cannot tell from where.

But I cannot tell from where
    He is calling out for aid !
Crying on the frightened air,
    Making everything afraid !

Making everything afraid!
　　Wrinkling up his little face!
As he cries again for aid;
　　—And I cannot find the place!

And I cannot find the place
　　Where his paw is in the snare!
Little one! Oh, little one!
　　I am searching everywhere!

James Stephens

THE GOAT PATHS

THE crooked paths go every way
　　Upon the hill—they wind about
　　Through the heather in and out
Of the quiet sunniness.
And there the goats, day after day,
　　Stray in sunny quietness,
Cropping here and cropping there,
　　As they pause and turn and pass,
Now a bit of heather spray,
　　Now a mouthful of the grass.

In the deeper sunniness,
　　In the place where nothing stirs,
Quietly in quietness,
　　In the quiet of the furze,
For a time they come and lie
Staring on the roving sky.

If you approach they run away,
　　They leap and stare, away they bound,
　　With a sudden angry sound,
To the sunny quietude;

Crouching down where nothing stirs
  In the silence of the furze,
Couching down again to brood
In the sunny solitude.

If I were as wise as they
  I would stray apart and brood,
I would beat a hidden way
Through the quiet heather spray
  To a sunny solitude;
And should you come I'd run away,
  I would make an angry sound,
  I would stare and turn and bound
To the deeper quietude,
  To the place where nothing stirs
  In the silence of the furze.

In that airy quietness
  I would think as long as they;
Through the quiet sunniness
  I would stray away to brood
By a hidden beaten way
  In a sunny solitude,

I would think until I found
  Something I can never find,
Something lying on the ground,
  In the bottom of my mind.

                    James Stephens

HATE

My enemy came nigh ;
And I
Stared fiercely in his face :
My lips went writhing back in a grimace,
And stern I watched him with a narrowed eye :

Then, as I turned away,
My enemy,
That bitter heart, and savage, said to me :

—Some day, when this is past ;
When all the arrows that we have are cast ;
We may ask one another why we hate ?
And fail to find a story to relate :
It may seem to us, then, a mystery
That we could hate each other—
Thus said he ; and did not turn away ;
Waiting to hear what I might have to say !

But I fled quickly : fearing, if I stayed,
I might have kissed him, as I would a maid.

James Stephens

THE HOUSE BEAUTIFUL

A naked house, a naked moor,
A shivering pool before the door,
A garden bare of flowers and fruit,
And poplars at the garden foot :
Such is the place that I live in,
Bleak without and bare within.

Yet shall your ragged moor receive
The incomparable pomp of eve,
And the cold glories of the dawn
Behind your shivering trees be drawn ;

And when the wind from place to place
Doth the unmoored cloud-galleons chase,
Your garden gloom and gleam again,
With leaping sun, with glancing rain.
Here shall the wizard moon ascend
The heavens, in the crimson end
Of day's declining splendour; here
The army of the stars appear.
The neighbour hollows, dry or wet,
Spring shall with tender flowers beset;
And oft the morning muser see
Larks rising from the broomy lea,
And every fairy wheel and thread
Of cobweb dew-bediamonded.
When daisies go, shall winter time
Silver the simple grass with rime;
Autumnal frosts enchant the pool
And make the cart-ruts beautiful;
And when snow-bright the moor expands,
How shall your children clap their hands!

To make this earth our hermitage,
A cheerful and a changeful page,
God's bright and intricate device
Of days and seasons doth suffice.

Robert Louis Stevenson

THE CELESTIAL SURGEON

IF I have faltered more or less
In my great task of happiness;
If I have moved among my race
And shown no glorious morning face;
If beams from happy human eyes
Have moved me not; if morning skies,

Books, and my food, and summer rain
Knocked on my sullen heart in vain :—
Lord, Thy most pointed pleasure take
And stab my spirit broad awake ;
Or, Lord, if too obdurate I,
Choose Thou, before that spirit die,
A piercing pain, a killing sin,
And to my dead heart run them in !

Robert Louis Stevenson

" HOME NO MORE HOME TO ME "

Home no more home to me, whither must I wander ?
   Hunger my driver, I go where I must.
Cold blows the winter wind over hill and heather ;
   Thick drives the rain, and my roof is in the dust.
Loved of wise men was the shade of my roof-tree,
   The true word of welcome was spoken in the door—
Dear days of old, with the faces in the firelight,
   Kind folks of old, you come again no more.

Home was home then, my dear, full of kindly faces,
   Home was home then, my dear, happy for the
     child.
Fire and the windows bright glittered on the moor-
     land ;
   Song, tuneful song, built a palace in the wild.
Now, when day dawns on the brow of the moorland,
   Lone stands the house, and the chimney-stone is
     cold.
Lone let it stand, now the friends are all departed,
   The kind hearts, the true hearts, that loved the
     place of old.

Spring shall come, come again, calling up the
    moor-fowl,
    Spring shall bring the sun and rain, bring the bees
      and flowers ;
Red shall the heather bloom over hill and valley,
    Soft flow the stream through the even-flowing
      hours ;
Fair the day shine as it shone on my childhood—
    Fair shine the day on the house with open door ;
Birds come and cry there and twitter in the chimney—
    But I go for ever and come again no more.

Robert Louis Stevenson

TO S. R. CROCKETT

BLOWS the wind to-day, and the sun and the rain
    are flying,
    Blows the wind on the moors to-day and now,
Where about the graves of the martyrs the whaups
    are crying,
    My heart remembers how !

Grey recumbent tombs of the dead in desert places,
    Standing-stones on the vacant wine-red moor,
Hills of sheep, and the homes of the silent vanquished
    races,
    And winds, austere and pure :

Be it granted me to behold you again in dying,
    Hills of home ! and to hear again the call ;
Hear about the graves of the martyrs the peewees
    crying,
    And hear no more at all.

Robert Louis Stevenson

REQUIEM

UNDER the wide and starry sky,
Dig the grave and let me lie.
Glad did I live and gladly die,
    And I laid me down with a will.

This be the verse you grave for me :
Here he lies where he longed to be,
Home is the sailor, home from sea,
    And the hunter home from the hill.
                Robert Louis Stevenson

THE BROKEN TRYST

THAT day a fire was in my blood ;
    I could have sung : joy wrapt me round ;
The men I met seemed all so good,
    I scarcely knew I trod the ground.

How easy seemed all toil ! I laughed
    To think that once I hated it.
The sunlight thrilled like wine, I quaffed
    Delight divine and infinite.

The very day was not too long ;
    I felt so patient ; I could wait,
Being certain. So, the hours in song
    Chimed out the minutes of my fate.

For she was coming, she, at last,
    I knew : I knew that bolts and bars
Could stay her not ; my heart throbbed fast,
    I was not more certain of the stars.

The twilight came, grew deeper; now
  The hour struck, minutes passed, and still
The passionate fervour of her vow
  Rang in my heart's ear audible.

I had no doubt at all: I knew
  That she would come, and I was then
Most certain, while the minutes flew:
  Ah, how I scorned all other men!

Next moment! Ah! it was—was not!
  I heard the stillness of the street.
Night came. The stars had not forgot.
  The moonlight fell about my feet.

So I rebuked my heart, and said:
  "Be still, for she is coming, see,
Next moment—coming. Ah, her tread,
  I hear her coming—it is she!"

And then a woman passed. The hour
  Rang heavily along the air.
I had no hope, I had no power
  To think—for thought was but despair.

A thing had happened. What? My brain
  Dared not so much as guess the thing.
And yet the sun would rise again
  Next morning! I stood marvelling.
                    Arthur Symons

14

HOME THOUGHTS IN LAVENTIE

GREEN gardens in Laventie !
  Soldiers only know the street
Where the mud is churned and splashed about
  By battle-wending feet ;
And yet beside one stricken house there is a glimpse
    of grass,
  Look for it when you pass.

Beyond the church whose pitted spire
  Seems balanced on a strand
Of swaying stone and tottering brick
  Two roofless ruins stand,
And here behind the wreckage where the back wall
    should have been
  We found a garden green.

The grass was never trodden on,
  The little path of gravel
Was overgrown with celandine,
  No other folk did travel
Along its weedy surface, but the nimble-footed
    mouse
  Running from house to house.

So all among the vivid blades
  Of soft and tender grass
We lay, nor heard the limber wheels
  That pass and ever pass,
In noisy continuity until their stony rattle
  Seems in itself a battle.

At length we rose up from this ease
  Of tranquil happy mind,
And searched the garden's little length
  A fresh pleasaunce to find ;
And there, some yellow daffodils and jasmine
    hanging high
  Did rest the tired eye.

The fairest and most fragrant
  Of the many sweets we found,
Was a little bush of Daphne flower
  Upon a grassy mound,
And so thick were the blossoms set and so divine
    the scent
  That we were well content.

Hungry for Spring I bent my head,
  The perfume fanned my face,
And all my soul was dancing,
  In that little lovely place,
Dancing with a measured step from wrecked and
    shattered towns
  Away . . . upon the Downs.

I saw green banks of daffodil,
  Slim poplars in the breeze,
Great tan-brown hares in gusty March
  A-courting on the leas ;
And meadows with their glittering streams, and
    silver scurrying dace,
  Home—what a perfect place.

                    Edward Wyndham Tennant

Belgium, *March,* 1916

LIGHTS OUT

I HAVE come to the borders of sleep,
The unfathomable deep
Forest where all must lose
Their way, however straight,
Or winding, soon or late ;
They cannot choose.

Many a road and track
That, since the dawn's first crack,
Up to the forest brink,
Deceived the travellers,
Suddenly now blurs,
And in they sink.

Here love ends,
Despair, ambition ends,
All pleasure and all trouble,
Although most sweet or bitter,
Here ends in sleep that is sweeter
Than tasks most noble.

There is not any book
Or face of dearest look
That I would not turn from now
To go into the unknown
I must enter and leave alone
I know not how.

The tall forest towers ;
Its cloudy foliage lowers
Ahead, shelf above shelf ;
Its silence I hear and obey
That I may lose my way
And myself.

Edward Thomas

WORDS

OUT of us all
That make rhymes,
Will you choose
Sometimes—
As the winds use
A crack in a wall
Or a drain,
Their joy or their pain
To whistle through—
Choose me,
You English words?

I know you:
You are light as dreams,
Tough as oak,
Precious as gold,
As poppies and corn,
Or an old cloak;
Sweet as our birds
To the ear,
As the burnet rose

In the heat
Of Midsummer:
Strange as the races
Of dead and unborn:
Strange and sweet
Equally,
And familiar,
To the eye,
As the dearest faces

That a man knows,
And as lost homes are:
But though older far
Than oldest yew,—
As our hills are, old,—
Worn new
Again and again:
Young as our streams
After rain:
And as dear
As the earth which you prove
That we love.

Make me content
With some sweetness
From Wales
Whose nightingales
Have no wings,—
From Wiltshire and Kent
And Herefordshire,
And the villages there,—
From the names, and the things
No less.
Let me sometimes dance
With you,
Or climb
Or stand perchance
In ecstasy,
Fixed and free
In a rhyme,
As poets do.

Edward Thomas

OUT IN THE DARK

Out in the dark over the snow
The fallow fawns invisible go
With the fallow doe;
And the winds blow
Fast as the stars are slow.

Stealthily the dark haunts round
And, when a lamp goes, without sound
At a swifter bound
Than the swiftest hound,
Arrives, and all else is drowned;

And I and star and wind and deer
Are in the dark together,—near,
Yet far,—and fear
Drums on my ear
In that sage company drear.

How weak and little is the light,
All the universe of sight,
Love and delight,
Before the might,
If you love it not, of night.

Edward Thomas

DAISY

Where the thistle lifts a purple crown
  Six foot out of the turf,
And the harebell shakes on the windy hill—
  O the breath of the distant surf!—

The hills look over on the South,
    And southward dreams the sea ;
And, with the sea-breeze hand in hand,
    Came innocence and she.

Where 'mid the gorse the raspberry
    Red for the gatherer springs,
Two children did we stray and talk
    Wise, idle, childish things.

She listen'd with big-lipped surprise,
    Breast-deep 'mid flower and spine :
Her skin was like a grape, whose veins
    Run snow instead of wine.

She knew not those sweet words she spake,
    Nor knew her own sweet way ;
But there's never a bird, so sweet a song
    Throng'd in whose throat that day !

O, there were flowers in Storrington
    On the turf and on the spray ;
But the sweetest flower on Sussex hills
    Was the Daisy-flower that day !

Her beauty smoothed earth's furrowed face !
    She gave me tokens three :—
A look, a word of her winsome mouth,
    And a wild raspberry.

A berry red, a guileless look,
    A still word,—strings of sand !
And yet they made my wild, wild heart
    Fly down to her little hand.

For, standing artless as the air,
    And candid as the skies,
She took the berries with her hand,
    And the love with her sweet eyes.

The fairest things have fleetest end,
    Their scent survives their close:
But the rose's scent is bitterness
    To him that loved the rose!

She looked a little wistfully,
    Then went her sunshine way:—
The sea's eye had a mist on it,
    And the leaves fell from the day.

She went her unremembering way,
    She went, and left in me
The pang of all the partings gone
    And partings yet to be.

She left me marvelling why my soul
    Was sad that she was glad;
At all the sadness in the sweet,
    The sweetness in the sad.

Still, still I seem'd to see her, still
    Look up with soft replies,
And take the berries with her hand,
    And the love with her lovely eyes.

Nothing begins, and nothing ends,
    That is not paid with moan;
For we are born in other's pain,
    And perish in our own.

                    Francis Thompson

TO A SNOWFLAKE

WHAT heart could have thought you ?—
Past our devisal
(O filigree petal !)
Fashioned so purely,
Fragilely, surely,
From what Paradisal
Imagineless metal,
Too costly for cost ?
Who hammered you, wrought you,
From argentine vapour ?—
" God was my shaper.
Passing surmisal,
He hammered, He wrought me,
From curled silver vapour,
To lust of His mind :—
Thou couldst not have thought me !
So purely, so palely,
Tinily, surely,
Mightily, frailly,
Insculped and embossed,
With His hammer of wind,
And His graver of frost."

Francis Thompson

IN NO STRANGE LAND

" The Kingdom of God is within you."

O WORLD invisible, we view thee,
    O world intangible, we touch thee,
O world unknowable, we know thee,
    Inapprehensible, we clutch thee !

Does the fish soar to find the ocean,
　The eagle plunge to find the air—
That we ask of the stars in motion
　If they have rumour of thee there?

Not where the wheeling systems darken,
　And our benumbed conceiving soars!—
The drift of pinions, would we hearken,
　Beats at our own clay-shuttered doors.

The angels keep their ancient places;—
　Turn but a stone, and start a wing!
'Tis ye, 'tis your estrangèd faces,
　That miss the many-splendoured thing.

But (when so sad thou canst not sadder)
　Cry;—and upon thy so sore loss
Shall shine the traffic of Jacob's ladder
　Pitched betwixt Heaven and Charing Cross.

Yea, in the night, my Soul, my daughter,
　Cry,—clinging Heaven by the hems;
And lo, Christ walking on the water,
　Not of Gennesareth, but Thames!
Francis Thompson

THE HOUND OF HEAVEN

I FLED Him, down the nights and down the days;
　I fled Him, down the arches of the years;
I fled Him, down the labyrinthine ways
　Of my own mind; and in the mist of tears
I hid from Him, and under running laughter.
　　　Up vistaed hopes I sped;
　　　And shot, precipitated,

Adown Titanic glooms of chasmèd fears,
From those strong Feet that followed, followed
    after.
        But with unhurrying chase,
        And unperturbèd pace,
    Deliberate speed, majestic instancy,
        They beat—and a Voice beat
        More instant than the Feet—
" All things betray thee, who betrayest Me."

      I pleaded, outlaw-wise,
By many a hearted casement, curtained red,
Trellised with intertwining charities ;
(For, though I knew His love Who followèd,
      Yet was I sore adread
Lest, having Him, I must have naught beside) ;
But, if one little casement parted wide,
The gust of His approach would clash it to.
Fear wist not to evade, as Love wist to pursue.
Across the margent of the world I fled,
    And troubled the gold gateways of the stars,
    Smiting for shelter on their clangèd bars ;
      Fretted to dulcet jars
And silvern chatter the pale ports o' the moon.
I said to Dawn : Be sudden—to Eve, Be soon ;
    With thy young skiey blossoms heap me over
      From this tremendous Lover—
Float thy vague veil about me, lest He see !
I tempted all His servitors, but to find
My own betrayal in their constancy,
In faith to Him their fickleness to me,
Their traitorous trueness, and their loyal deceit.
To all swift things for swiftness did I sue ;
    Clung to the whistling mane of every wind.
      But whether they swept, smoothly fleet,

The long savannahs of the blue;
  Or whether, Thunder-driven,
 They clanged his chariot 'thwart a heaven,
Plashy with flying lightnings round the spurn
   o' their feet :—
Fear wist not to evade as Love wist to pursue.
  Still with unhurrying chase,
  And unperturbèd pace,
 Deliberate speed, majestic instancy,
  Came on the following Feet,
  And a Voice above their beat—
" Naught shelters thee, who wilt not shelter Me."

I sought no more that after which I strayed
  In face of man or maid;
But still within the little children's eyes
 Seems something, something that replies,
They at least are for me, surely for me!
I turned me to them very wistfully;
But, just as their young eyes grew sudden fair
 With dawning answers there,
Their angel plucked them from me by the hair.
" Come then, ye other children, Nature's—share
With me " (said I) " your delicate fellowship;
  Let me greet you lip to lip,
  Let me twine with you caresses,
   Wantoning
  With our Lady-Mother's vagrant tresses,
   Banqueting
  With her in her wind-walled palace,
  Underneath her azured daïs,
  Quaffing as your taintless way is,
   From a chalice
Lucent-weeping out of the dayspring."

So it was done:
I in their delicate fellowship was one—
Drew the bolt of Nature's secrecies.
> *I* knew all the swift importings
> On the wilful face of skies;
> I knew how the clouds arise
> Spumèd of the wild sea-snortings;
>> All that's born or dies
> Rose and drooped with; made them shapers
Of mine own moods, or wailful or divine;
> With them joyed and was bereaven.
> I was heavy with the even,
> When she lit her glimmering tapers
> Round the day's dead sanctities.
> I laughed in the morning's eyes.
I triumphed and I saddened with all weather,
> Heaven and I wept together,
And its sweet tears were salt with mortal mine;
Against the red throb of its sunset-heart
> I laid my own to beat,
> And share commingling heat;
But not by that, by that, was eased my human smart.
In vain my tears were wet on Heaven's grey cheek.
For ah! we know not wha̅ each other says
> These things and I; in sound *I* speak—
Their sound is but their stir, they speak by silences.
Nature, poor stepdame, cannot slake my drouth;
> Let her, if she would owe me,
Drop yon blue bosom-veil of sky, and show me
> The breasts o' her tenderness:
Never did any milk of hers once bless
> My thirsting mouth.

Nigh and nigh draws the chase
With unperturbèd pace,
Deliberate speed, majestic instancy;
And past those noisèd Feet
A voice comes yet more fleet—
" Lo! naught contents thee, who content'st
not Me."

Naked I wait Thy love's uplifted stroke!
My harness piece by piece Thou hast hewn from me,
And smitten me to my knee;
I am defenceless utterly.
I slept, methinks, and woke,
And, slowly gazing, find me stripped in sleep.
In the rash lustihead of my young powers,
I shook the pillaring hours
And pulled my life upon me; grimed with smears,
I stand amid the dust o' the mounded years—
My mangled youth lies dead beneath the heap.
My days have crackled and gone up in smoke,
Have puffed and burst as sun-starts on a stream.
Yea, faileth now even dream
The dreamer, and the lute the lutanist;
Even the linked fantasies, in whose blossomy twist
I swung the earth a trinket at my wrist,
Are yielding; cords of all too weak account
For earth with heavy griefs so overplussed.
Ah! is Thy love indeed
A weed, albeit an amaranthine weed,
Suffering no flowers except its own to mount?
Ah! must—
Designer infinite!—
Ah! must Thou char the wood ere Thou canst
limn with it?

My freshness spent its wavering shower i' the dust;
And now my heart is as a broken fount,
Wherein tear-drippings stagnate, spilt down ever
    From the dank thoughts that shiver
Upon the sighful branches of my mind.
    Such is; what is to be?
The pulp so bitter, how shall taste the rind?
I dimly guess what Time in mists confounds;
Yet ever and anon a trumpet sounds
From the hid battlements of Eternity;
Those shaken mists a space unsettle, then
Round the half glimpsèd turrets slowly wash again.
    But not ere him who summoneth
    I first have seen, enwound
With glooming robes purpureal, cypress-crowned;
His name I know, and what his trumpet saith.
Whether man's heart or life it be which yields
    Thee harvest, must Thy harvest-fields
    Be dunged with rotten death?

    Now of that long pursuit
    Comes on at hand the bruit;
  That Voice is round me like a bursting sea:
    " And is thy earth so marred,
    Shattered in shard on shard?
  Lo, all things fly thee, for thou fliest Me!
  Strange, piteous, futile thing,
Wherefore should any set thee love apart?
Seeing none but I makes much of naught " (He said),
" And human love needs human meriting:
    How hast thou merited—
Of all man's clotted clay the dingiest clot?
    Alack, thou knowest not
How little worthy of any love thou art!

Whom wilt thou find to love ignoble thee,
  Save Me, save only Me ?
All which I took from thee I did but take,
  Not for thy harms,
But just that thou might'st seek it in My arms.
  All which thy child's mistake
Fancies as lost, I have stored for thee at home :
  Rise, clasp My hand, and come ! "

  Halts by me that footfall :
  Is my gloom, after all,
Shade of His hand, outstretched caressingly ?
  " Ah, fondest, blindest, weakest,
  I am He Whom thou seekest !
Thou dravest love from thee, who dravest Me."

      Francis Thompson

O DREAMY, GLOOMY, FRIENDLY TREES

O DREAMY, gloomy, friendly Trees,
 I came along your narrow track
To bring my gifts unto your knees,
 And gifts did you give back ;
For when I brought this heart that burns—
 These thoughts that bitterly repine—
And laid them here among the ferns
 And the hum of boughs divine,
Ye, vastest breathers of the air,
 Shook down with slow and mighty poise
Your coolness on the human care,
 Your wonder on its toys,
Your greenness on the heart's despair,
 Your darkness on its noise.

      Herbert Trench

15

ECSTASY

I saw a frieze on whitest marble drawn
Of boys who sought for shells along the shore,
Their white feet shedding pallor in the sea,
The shallow sea, the spring-time sea of green
That faintly creamed against the cold, smooth
    pebbles.

The air was thin, their limbs were delicate,
The wind had graven their small eager hands
To feel the forests and the dark nights of Asia
Behind the purple bloom of the horizon,
Where sails would float and slowly melt away.

Their naked, pure, and grave, unbroken silence
Filled the soft air as gleaming, limpid water
Fills a spring sky those days when rain is lying
In shattered bright pools on the wind-dried roads,
And their sweet bodies were wind-purified.

One held a shell unto his shell-like ear
And there was music carven in his face,
His eyes half-closed, his lips just breaking open
To catch the lulling, mazy, coralline roar
Of numberless caverns filled with singing seas.

And all of them were hearkening as to singing
Of far-off voices thin and delicate,
Voices too fine for any mortal wind
To blow into the whorls of mortal ears—
And yet those sounds flowed from their grave,
    sweet faces.

And as I looked I heard that delicate music,
And I became as grave, as calm, as still
As those carved boys. I stood upon that shore,
I felt the cool sea dream around my feet,
My eyes were staring at the far horizon;

And the wind came and purified my limbs,
And the stars came and set within my eyes,
And snowy clouds rested upon my shoulders,
And the blue sky shimmered deep within me,
And I sang like a carven pipe of music.

W. J. Turner

THE PRINCESS

THE stone-grey roses by the desert's rim
Are soft-edged shadows on the moonlit sand,
Grey are the broken walls of Conchubar,
That haunt of nightingales, whose voices are
Fountains that bubble in the dream-soft Moon.

Shall the Gazelles with moonbeam pale bright feet
Entering the vanished gardens sniff the air—
Some scent may linger of that ancient time,
Musician's song, or poet's passionate rhyme,
The Princess dead, still wandering love-sick there.

A Princess pale and cold as mountain snow,
In cool, dark chambers sheltered from the sun,
With long dark lashes and small delicate hands:
All Persia sighed to kiss her small red mouth
Until they buried her in shifting sand.

And the Gazelles shall flit by in the Moon
And never shake the frail Tree's lightest leaves,
And moonlight roses perfume the pale Dawn,
Until the scarlet life that left her lips
Gathers its shattered beauty in the sky.

W. J. Turner

ROMANCE

WHEN I was but thirteen or so
   I went into a golden land,
Chimborazo, Cotopaxi
   Took me by the hand.

My father died, my brother too,
   They passed like fleeting dreams,
I stood where Popocatapetl
   In the sunlight gleams.

I dimly heard the master's voice
   And boys far-off at play,
Chimborazo, Cotopaxi
   Had stolen me away.

I walked in a great golden dream
   To and fro from school—
Shining Popocatapetl
   The dusty streets did rule.

I walked home with a gold dark boy,
   And never a word I'd say,
Chimborazo, Cotopaxi
   Had taken my speech away:

I gazed entranced upon his face
   Fairer than any flower—

O shining Popocatapetl,
   It was thy magic hour:

The houses, people, traffic seemed
   Thin fading dreams by day,
Chimborazo, Cotopaxi
   They had stolen my soul away!

                              W. J. Turner

THE CHOICE

WHEN skies are blue and days are bright,
A kitchen-garden's my delight,
Set round with rows of decent box
And blowsy girls of hollyhocks.

Before the lark his Lauds hath done
And ere the corncrake's southward gone;
Before the thrush good-night hath said
And the young Summer's put to bed.

The currant-bushes' spicy smell,
Homely and honest, likes me well.
The while on strawberries I feast,
And raspberries the sun hath kissed.

Beans all a-blowing by a row
Of hives that great with honey go,
With mignonette and heaths to yield
The plundering bee his honey-field.

Sweet herbs in plenty, blue borage
And the delicious mint and sage,
Rosemary, marjoram, and rue,
And thyme to scent the winter through.

Here are small apples growing round,
And apricots all golden-gowned,
And plums that presently will flush
And show their bush a Burning Bush.

Cherries in nets against the wall,
Where Master Thrush his madrigal
Sings, and makes oath, a churl is he
Who grudges cherries for a fee.

Lavender, sweet-briar, orris. Here
Shall Beauty make her pomander,
Her sweet balls for to lay in clothes
That wrap her as the leaves the rose.

Take roses red and lilies white,
A kitchen-garden's my delight;
Its gillyflowers and phlox and cloves,
And its tall cote of irised doves.

Katharine Tynan

LACRIMÆ MUSARUM

(6th October, 1892: *Tennyson's Death*)

Low, like another's, lies the laurelled head:
The life that seemed a perfect song is o'er:
Carry the last great bard to his last bed.
Land that he loved, thy noblest voice is mute.
Land that he loved, that loved him ! nevermore
Meadow of thine, smooth lawn or wild sea-shore,
Gardens of odorous bloom and tremulous fruit,
Or woodlands old, like Druid couches spread,
The master's feet shall tread.
Death's little rift hath rent the faultless lute:
The singer of undying songs is dead.

Lo, in this season pensive-hued and grave,
While fades and falls the doomed, reluctant leaf
From withered Earth's fantastic coronal,
With wandering sighs of forest and of wave
Mingles the murmur of a people's grief
For him whose leaf shall fade not, neither fall.
He hath fared forth, beyond these suns and showers.
For us, the autumn glow, the autumn flame,
And soon the winter silence shall be ours:
Him the eternal spring of fadeless fame
Crowns with no mortal flowers.

What needs his laurel our ephemeral tears,
To save from visitation of decay?
Not in this temporal light alone, that bay
Blooms, nor to perishable mundane ears
Sings he with lips of transitory clay.
Rapt though he be from us,
Virgil salutes him, and Theocritus;
Catullus, mightiest-brained Lucretius, each
Greets him, their brother, on the Stygian beach;
Proudly a gaunt right hand doth Dante reach;
Milton and Wordsworth bid him welcome home;
Keats, on his lips the eternal rose of youth,
Doth in the name of Beauty that is Truth
A Kinsman's love beseech;
Coleridge, his locks aspersed with fairy foam,
Calm Spenser, Chaucer suave,
His equal friendship crave:
And godlike spirits hail him guest, in speech
Of Athens, Florence, Weimar, Stratford, Rome.

Nay, he returns to regions whence he came.
Him doth the spirit divine
Of universal loveliness reclaim.

All nature is his shrine.
Seek him henceforward in the wind and sea,
In earth's and air's emotion or repose,
In every star's august serenity,
And in the rapture of the flaming rose.
There seek him if ye would not seek in vain,
There, in the rhythm and music of the Whole;
Yea, and for ever in the human soul
Made stronger and more beauteous by his strain.

For lo! creation's self is one great choir,
And what is nature's order but the rhyme
Whereto in holiest unanimity
All things with all things move unfalteringly,
Infolded and communal from their prime?
Who shall expound the mystery of the lyre?
In far retreats of elemental mind
Obscurely comes and goes
The imperative breath of song, that as the wind
Is trackless, and oblivious whence it blows.
Demand of lilies wherefore they are white,
Extort her crimson secret from the rose,
But ask not of the Muse that she disclose
The meaning of the riddle of her might:
Somewhat of all things sealed and recondite,
Save the enigma of herself, she knows.
The master could not tell, with all his lore,
Wherefore he sang, or whence the mandate sped:
Ev'n as the linnet sings, so I, he said:
Ah, rather as the imperial nightingale,
That held in trance the ancient Attic shore,
And charms the ages with the notes that o'er
All woodland chants immortally prevail!
And now, from our vain plaudits greatly fled,

He with diviner silence dwells instead,
And on no earthly sea with transient roar,
Unto no earthly airs, he trims his sail,
But far beyond our vision and our hail
Is heard for ever and is seen no more.

No more, O never now,
Lord of the lofty and the tranquil brow,
Shall men behold those wizard locks where Time
Let fall no wintry rime.
Once, in his youth obscure,
The maker of this verse, that shall endure
By splendour of its theme which cannot die,
Beheld thee eye to eye,
And touched through thee the hand
Of every hero of thy race divine,
Ev'n to the sire of all the laurelled line,
The sightless wanderer on the Ionian strand.
Yea, I beheld thee, and behold thee yet:
Thou hast forgotten, but can I forget?
Are not thy words all goldenly impressed
On memory's palimpsest?
I hear the utterance of thy sovereign tongue,
I tread the floor thy hallowing feet have trod ;
I see the hands a nation's lyre that strung,
The eyes that looked through life and gazed on God.

The seasons change, the winds they shift and veer ;
The grass of yesteryear
Is dead ; the birds depart, the groves decay :
Empires dissolve and peoples disappear :
Song passes not away.
Captains and conquerors leave a little dust,

THEOCRITUS

A Villanelle

O Singer of Persephone!
In the dim meadows desolate
Dost thou remember Sicily?

Still through the ivy flits the bee
Where Amaryllis lies in state;
O Singer of Persephone!

Simætha calls on Hecate
And hears the wild dogs at the gate;
Dost thou remember Sicily?

Still by the light and laughing sea
Poor Polypheme bemoans his fate;
O Singer of Persephone!

And still in boyish rivalry
Young Daphnis challenges his mate
Dost thou remember Sicily?

Slim Lacon keeps a goat for thee,
For thee the jocund shepherds wait;
O Singer of Persephone!
Dost thou remember Sicily?

Oscar Wilde

THERE ARE SWEET FIELDS

There are sweet fields that lie
Under the mountains,
Where life runs pleasantly
Like little fountains.

There has the sun forgot
His cruel fire,
And the strong air wanders not
From the craig-heads higher.

There may the grey heart sing
How Youth was stronger,
And love a far-off thing
That hurts no longer.

Iolo Aneurin Williams

WHEN YOU ARE OLD

WHEN you are old and grey and full of sleep,
And nodding by the fire, take down this book,
And slowly read; and dream of the soft look
Your eyes had once, and of their shadows deep;

How many loved your moments of glad grace,
And loved your beauty with love false or true;
But one man loved the pilgrim soul in you,
And loved the sorrows of your changing face;

And bending down beside the glowing bars
Murmur, a little sadly, how love fled,
And paced upon the mountains overhead,
And hid his face amid a crown of stars.

W. B. Yeats

AEDH WISHES FOR THE CLOTHS OF HEAVEN

HAD I the heavens' embroidered cloths,
Enwrought with golden and silver light,
The blue and the dim and the dark cloths
Of night and light and the half light,

Bow down, archangels, in your dim abode :
  Before you were, or any hearts to beat,
  Weary and kind one lingered by His seat ;
He made the world to be a grassy road
  Before her wandering feet.

W. B. Yeats

THE WHITE BIRDS

I would that we were, my beloved, white birds on
    the foam of the sea !
We tire of the flame of the meteor, before it can
    fade and flee ;
And the flame of the blue star of twilight, hung
    low on the rim of the sky,
Has awaked in our hearts, my beloved, a sadness
    that may not die.

A weariness comes from those dreamers, dew-
    dabbled, the lily and rose ;
Ah, dream not of them, my beloved, the flame of
    the meteor that goes,
Or the flame of the blue star that lingers hung low
    in the fall of the dew :
For I would we were changed to white birds on the
    wandering foam : I and you !

I am haunted by numberless islands, and many
    a Danaan shore,
Where Time would surely forget us, and Sorrow
    come near us no more ;
Soon far from the rose and the lily, and free of the
    flames would we be,
Were we only white birds, my beloved, buoyed
    out on the foam of the sea !

W. B. Yeats

DOWN BY THE SALLEY GARDENS

DOWN by the salley gardens my love and I did
meet ;
She passed the salley gardens with little snow-
white feet.
She bid me take love easy, as the leaves grow on
the tree ;
But I, being young and foolish, with her would
not agree.

In a field by the river my love and I did stand,
And on my leaning shoulder she laid her snow-
white hand.
She bid me take life easy, as the grass grows on
the weirs ;
But I was young and foolish, and now am full of
tears.

W. B. Yeats

LAKE ISLE OF INNISFREE

I WILL arise and go now, and go to Innisfree,
   And a small cabin build there, of clay and
     wattles made :
Nine bean rows will I have there, a hive for the
honey bee,
   And live alone in the bee-loud glade.

And I shall have some peace there, for peace comes
     dropping slow,
   Dropping from the veils of the morning to where
     the cricket sings ;
There midnight's all a glimmer, and noon a purple
     glow,
   And evening full of the linnet's wings.

16

I will arise and go now, for always night and day
  I hear lake water lapping with low sounds by
      the shore ;
While I stand on the roadway, or on the pave-
    ments grey
  I hear it in the deep heart's core.

W. B. Yeats

THE SORROW OF LOVE

THE quarrel of the sparrows in the eaves,
  The full round moon and the star-laden sky,
And the loud song of the ever-singing leaves
  Had hid away earth's old and weary cry.

And then you came with those red mournful lips,
  And with you came the whole of the world's tears,
And all the sorrows of her labouring ships,
  And all the burden of her myriad years.

And now the sparrows warring in the eaves,
  The crumbling moon, the white stars in the sky,
And the loud chanting of the unquiet leaves
  Are shaken with earth's old and weary cry.

W. B. Yeats

PROTHALAMION

WHEN the evening came my love said to me :
  Let us go into the garden now that the sky is cool,
The garden of black hellebore and rosemary,
  Where wild woodruff spills in a milky pool.

Low we passed in the twilight, for the wavering heat
  Of day had waned, and round that shaded plot
Of secret beauty the thickets clustered sweet :
  Here is heaven, our hearts whispered, but our
    lips spake not.

Between that old garden and seas of lazy foam
    Gloomy and beautiful alleys of trees arise
With spire of cypress and dreamy beechen dome,
    So dark that our enchanted sight knew nothing
        but the skies

Veiled with a soft air, drench'd in the roses' musk
    Or the dusky, dark carnation's breath of clove :
No stars burned in their deeps, but through the dusk
    I saw my love's eyes, and they were brimmed
        with love.

No star their secret ravished, no wasting moon
    Mocked the sad transience of those eternal hours :
Only the soft, unseeing heaven of June,
    The ghosts of great trees, and the sleeping flowers.

For doves that crooned in the leafy noonday now
    Were silent ;   the night-jar sought his secret
        covers,
Nor even a mild sea-whisper moved   a creaking
        bough—
    Was ever a silence deeper made for lovers ?

Was ever a moment meeter made for love ?
    Beautiful are your close lips beneath my kiss ;
And all your yielding sweetness beautiful—
    Oh, never in all the world was such a night as
        this !

                            Francis Brett Young

FEBRUARY

THE robin on my lawn,
He was the first to tell
How, in the frozen dawn,
This miracle befell,
Waking the meadows white
With hoar, the iron road

Agleam with splintered light,
And ice where water flowed :
Till, when the low sun drank
Those milky mists that cloak
Hanger and hollied bank,
The winter world awoke
To hear the feeble bleat
Of lambs on the downland farms :
A blackbird whistled sweet ;
Old beeches moved their arms
Into a mellow haze
Aerial, newly-born :
And I, alone, agaze,
Stood waiting for the thorn
To break in blossoms white,
Or burst in a green flame. . . .
So, in a single night,
Fair February came,
Bidding my lips to sing
Or whisper their surprise,
With all the joy of spring
And morning in her eyes.

Francis Brett Young

THE LEANING ELM

BEFORE my window, in days of winter hoar,
Huddled a mournful wood :
Smooth pillars of beech, domed chestnut, sycamore,
In stony sleep they stood :
But you, unhappy elm, the angry west
Had chosen from the rest,
Flung broken on your brothers' branches bare,
And left you leaning there

So dead that, when the breath of winter cast
Wild snow upon the blast,
The other living branches, downward bowed,
Shook free their crystal shroud
And shed upon your blackened trunk beneath
Their livery of death. . . .

On windless nights between the beechen bars
I watched cold stars
Throb whitely in the sky, and dreamily
Wondered if any life lay locked in thee :
If still the hidden sap secretly moved
As water in the icy winterbourne
Floweth unheard :
And half I pitied you your trance forlorn :
You could not hear, I thought, the voice of any bird,
The shadowy cries of bats in dim twilight
Or cool voices of owls crying by night. . . .
Hunting by night under the hornèd moon :
Yet half I envied you your wintry swoon,
Till, on this morning mild, the sun, new-risen
Steals from his misty prison ;
The frozen fallows glow, the black trees shaken
In a clear flood of sunlight vibrating awaken :
And lo, your ravaged bole, beyond belief
Slenderly fledged anew with tender leaf
As pale as those twin vanes that break at last
In a tiny fan above the black beech-mast
Where no blade springeth green
But pallid bells of the shy helleborine.
What is this ecstasy that overwhelms
The dreaming earth ?   See, the embrownèd elms
Crowding purple distances warm the depths of the
          wood :

A new-born wind tosses their tassels brown,
His white clouds dapple the down;
Into a green flame bursting the hedgerows stand;
Soon, with banners flying, Spring will walk the
　　land. . . .

There is no day for thee, my soul, like this,
No spring of lovely words. Nay, even the kiss
Of mortal love that maketh man divine
This light cannot outshine:
Nay, even poets, they whose frail hands catch
The shadow of vanishing beauty, may not match
This leafy ecstasy. Sweet words may cull
Such magical beauty as time may not destroy;
But we, alas, are not more beautiful:
We cannot flower in beauty as in joy.
We sing, our musèd words are sped, and then
Poets are only men
Who age, and toil, and sicken. . . . This maim'd
　　tree
May stand in leaf when I have ceased to be.
　　　　　　　　　　　　　Francis Brett Young

CHRISTMAS

A BOY was born at Bethlehem
　　that knew the haunts of Galilee.
He wandered on Mount Lebanon,
　　and learned to love each forest tree.

But I was born at Marlborough,
　　and love the homely faces there;
and for all other men besides
　　'tis little love I have to spare.

I should not mind to die for them,
   my own dear downs, my comrades true.
But that great heart of Bethlehem,
   he died for men he never knew.

And yet, I think, at Golgotha,
   as Jesus' eyes were closed in death,
they saw with love most passionate
   the village street at Nazareth.

H.M.S. *Iron Duke*, 1914

                 E. Hilton Young

THE CRAGSMAN

In this short span
between my finger tips on the smooth edge
and these tense feet cramped to the crystal ledge
I hold the life of man.
Consciously I embrace
arched from the mountain rock on which I stand
to the firm limit of my lifted hand
the front of time and space :—
    For what is there in all the world for me
      but what I know and see ?
    And what remains of all I see and know,
      if I let go ?

With this full breath
bracing my sinews as I upward move
boldly reliant to the rift above
I measure life from death.
With each strong thrust
I feel all motion and all vital force

borne on my strength and hazarding their course
in my self-trust :—

    There is no movement of what kind it be
        but has its source in me ;
    and should these muscles falter to release
        motion itself must cease.

In these two eyes
that search the splendour of the earth, and seek
the sombre mysteries on plain and peak,
all vision wakes and dies.
With these my ears
that listen for the sound of lakes asleep
and love the larger rumour from the deep,
the eternal hears :—

    For all of beauty that this life can give
        lives only while I live ;
    and with the light my hurried vision lends
        all beauty ends.

Geoffrey Winthrop Young

INDEX OF FIRST LINES